THE COMPLETE RAPIER

— Workbook —

Guy Windsor

Published by Spada Press

© Guy Windsor and Spada Press 2021

No part of this book may be reproduced or transmitted in any form
or by any other means without permission in writing from the author,
except by a reviewer who wishes to quote brief passages in connection
with a review written for insertion in a magazine, newspaper or broadcast

ISBN 978-952-7157-53-4 The Complete Rapier Workbook LH paperback

This book belongs to:

....

Date begun: ....

Date completed: ....

TABLE OF CONTENTS

THE RAPIER

Part I: Beginners

— Workbook —

Guy Windsor

Published by Spada Press

© Guy Windsor and Spada Press 2018

ISBN: 978-952-7157-44-2 R1.1 Right Handers
ISBN: 978-952-7157-45-9 R1.2 Left Handers

This book belongs to:

…………………………………………………………………………………

Date begun: …………………………..

Date completed: ………………………….

TABLE OF CONTENTS

INTRODUCTION

One of the hardest questions to answer in any martial art is "where do you start?" Every beginner is different, and every beginners' course has to take into account the physical and mental experience and aptitudes of the individuals on the course. This book is based on my experience of running dozens of beginners' courses for hundreds of different students. The point of this course is to give beginners a thorough basic grounding in one specific historical style of rapier fencing. The point of this workbook is to give beginners a really clear path through the first few steps, and for less experienced instructors a template to follow or to adapt for creating their own courses.

Rather than static images, I've chosen to illustrate this book with video clips. These come from my various online resources, such as the Essential Rapier Course, the Breathing Course, and my Syllabus Wiki. If a picture is worth a thousand words, then surely a video is worth a thousand pictures (which, of course, videos are made up of). As every exercise is introduced, I provide an easy-to-type redirect link to the video file, and a QR code for the same link, which currently point to my youtube channel. You may want to download a QR reader onto your phone if you don't have one already. If you want to download the videos to store them locally (ideal for training in places with no internet coverage), you will find links to them on this page of my website:

I am assuming the following things:

1. you are physically and mentally healthy enough to begin training

2. you are a beginner with little or no experience, or an inexperienced instructor

3. you want to actually practise with the sword

4. you want to practise in a historically authentic style

5. you have at least one friend to train with

6. you have some basic equipment: a training sword and a mask per person, a pen and a smartphone (or other device for watching internet videos)

7. you rightly believe that the rapier is the most elegant, most sophisticated, perfect sword (or at least are willing to believe it long enough to read the book).

If that isn't you, then this might be the wrong book for you. There's a list of my other works at the end of this book.

Beginners' courses are usually funnels or filters. Schools or groups that are most interested in winning tournaments tend to filter out students that are unlikely to do so. They do this by making the course physically demanding and competitive, so only fit, competitive, people make it through. I prefer the funnel approach: I think the beginners' course should be attractive to as wide a range of people as possible, and it should provide a natural entry point into regular swordsmanship training. I have written this workbook from that perspective. This book is based on one particular course I taught (and took detailed notes on) in 2015.

A Note to Instructors

Before you can use this course as a template for creating your own, you need to establish a few things:

1. What is your course for? Ours was intended to ease students in to our regular Wednesday night rapier class. In other words, it was not intended as a survey course, nor did its members expect to be master fencers by the end of it. Neither were we trying to filter out those students unlikely to win tournaments.

2. Who is it for? Ours was populated mostly by students who had at least a few months of training at our school, so they were familiar with certain concepts, and with courtesies such as salutes. This meant that we could cover a lot of material very fast. If everyone present was a total newbie, I expect this much material would take about 8 weeks, not 5.

3. Teaching swordsmanship has been my full-time job for 15 years. When I was starting out, I was amazed by how much stuff more experienced teachers could somehow cover in a short class, without baffling the students. Looking back, I can see that over time I have become much more efficient at getting students to absorb material. If you have less experience, then you will probably find that you need to break this material up further, and cover less in a single session. Take your time.

4. I will be adding notes on teaching this material throughout the book, but this is not about how to teach. I cover how to teach a basic class in my book The Theory and Practice of Historical Martial Arts.

Experienced fencers or instructors will have their own ideas about what belongs in a beginners' course, and in what order the material should be presented. I have never taught the same beginners' course twice; it is always influenced by the students present, and my current interests and theories. But I would say that no Capoferro-style rapier beginners' course would be complete without the following components:

* The four guards
* the lunge
* stepping forwards and back
* stringering
* attack by disengage
* Plate 7
* Plate 16.

Plus, of course, any prerequisites those actions may require, such as how to do a disengage, discussion of tempo, and so on.

The reason I spend so much time on plates 7 and 16 is because taken together, they form a kind of zip file for the system. To be able to do both plates requires:

* Stringering
* attack by disengage,
* parry riposte in one tempo
* feint
* parry riposte in two tempi
* thrusts
* cuts
* beat attack.

That is a very comprehensive list; the only obvious omission is the avoidances, which tend to require more athleticism than the average beginner is ready for. Once the student has these two plates, they can expand on any one of those topics: they could take the second parry riposte in two tempi option from Plate 7 and use that as a starting point to study the cuts, for instance.

A Note to Left-handers

We know for certain that people in this period (early 1600s) did fence left-handed, not least because Capoferro himself gives specific instructions on how to kill left-handers! (See Plate 38, for example). If you are left-handed:

For solo training, just reverse all left-right instructions.
For pair drills with a fellow lefty, reverse all left-right instructions, but keep inside and outside instructions the same.
For pair drills with a right-hander (curse them), reverse your left-right instructions, but also reverse inside/outside instructions too. I'll give some examples as they arise in the booklet.

In my experience, the last thing that beginners need is a pile of information to wade through before they get to the actions. It is much more effective to get you doing things with the bare minimum of explanation, and then when you have some practical sense of what the actions are, give you the theory. I've followed that principle in this book, and resisted my usual tendency to explain everything in great depth. I think that once you have worked through this book, you will find reading a more in-depth work (like my *Duellist's Companion*) much more rewarding, because you will have a basic understanding already in place.

Please note also that I have produced two versions of this book; if you're left-handed, you'll find writing up notes much easier in the version of the book laid out for left-handers. If you've bought the wrong one by accident, email me and I'll send you the print file for the other version. Sadly left-handers still read left-to-right, the same as everyone else in this culture, so putting the notes on the left-hand side does not create a perfectly seamless reading experience, but I've done my best.

Equipment

For this level you will need only a training rapier and a fencing mask. If you have more equipment feel free to use it, but in keeping with the 'funnel' idea, I like to keep requirements for the beginners' course to a minimum.

Capoferro's system works best with a sword that weighs between 1kg and 1.6kg (2.0—3.5 lb), with the point of balance between 6 and 15 cm (2.5—6 inches) in front of the crossguard, a complex hilt that allows you to put your forefinger over the crossguard safely, and a blade length from crossguard to point of at least 97 cm (38") (for short people), up to a maximum of about 114 cm (45").

Capoferro himself tells us, in Chapter III: The Division of Fencing That is Posed in the Knowledge of the Sword, section 36:

"Therefore the sword has to be twice as long as the arm, and as much as my extraordinary pace, which length corresponds equally to that which is from my armpit down to the sole of my foot." (Translation by William Wilson and Jherek Swanger).

I have never met anyone for whom those three measurements were the same, and in my book *The Duellist's Companion* I worked them out like so:

"My arm is 52 cm, shoulder to wrist; my lunge about 120 cm from heel to heel, and it is about 140 cm from my foot to my armpit when standing. When standing on guard, it is about 115cm from foot to armpit. When in the lunge, it is about 104 cm from foot to armpit. Also, it is not clear whether he refers to the length of the blade, or of the whole sword.

If we resort to the unreliable practice of measuring the illustrations, in the picture of the lunge, the sword blade is 73 mm, the arm from wrist to armpit 37 mm, and the line G (front heel to front armpit) 55 mm. The distance between the feet is 67 mm.

So, the measurement most consistent with the text would appear to be the length of the arm, from wrist to armpit, as it approximately correlates to half the length of the blade.

Given this as a guide, my blade ought to be 104 cm or about 41" long from the guard to the point."

Specifications Summary:
Hilt type: a full complex hilt; either swept, Pappenheim, or cup.
Total Length: 45 - 53 inches, 114 - 135cm
Blade Length: 38 - 45 inches, 96 - 114cm
Weight: 2.8-3.5lb, 1.25 - 1.6kg
Point of Balance: 2.5 - 6 inches, 6 - 15cm from the cross.

For more information on choosing a sword, go to https://guywindsor.net/blog/freebook-2/ and get my free booklet *Choosing a Sword*.

Using this Workbook

Work through the book, annotating as you go, and you will finish it with a solid basic understanding of Capoferro's rapier system, in theory and in practice.

I have divided the book up into four classes of about 90 minutes each. You may well find that without a live instructor there you may need more time to go through the material. It is better to go slower and really get to grips with the material you are working on, than to try to cram too much material into the allotted time. Some folk work in 30-minute blocks, some in three hours; it's impossible to pick a division that works for everyone. Please treat the division into classes as a suggestion, not a rule!

It is very important that you clearly distinguish between blocked practice and play. In blocked practice you will set up a drill choreographically, and practise it as accurately as you can. This is an essential starting point - it teaches you *what to practise*. By itself though, it isn't really practice at all. For serious skill development we have many approaches, the most important of which is play. I introduce play in the very first class, and you will be learning how to play usefully throughout this course. Just be advised that "play" does not equal "do what the hell you like". Every game has rules, and to use the games effectively you must pay attention to those rules and play within them. For a detailed breakdown of how to develop skill, there's a whole chapter on it in The Theory and Practice of Historical Martial Arts, and I plan to cover it in a later instalment of this series.

Safety

When training with weapons you hold your partner's life in your hands. This is a sacred trust and must not be abused.

Disclaimer: I accept no responsibility of any kind for injuries you sustain while you are not under my direct personal supervision. During this course you will be taught how to create safe training drills, and I am certain that if you follow the instructions there is a very low likelihood of injury. But if I am not there in person to create and sustain a safe training environment, I cannot be held responsible for any accidents that may occur.

Principles

The basic principles of safe training are:

1. Respect: for the Art, your training partners, the weapons, and yourself.

2. Caution: assume everything is dangerous unless you have reason to believe otherwise.

3. Know your limits. Just because it's safe for somebody else, does not necessarily mean it's safe for you. Never train or fence when you are tired, angry, or in any state of mind or body that makes accidents and injuries more likely.

Most groups that keep going for more than a year have a pretty good set of safety guidelines in place. Make sure you know what they are, and follow them.

My senior students routinely train with sharp swords, often with no protection. That's not as dangerous as it sounds, when you remember that they have been training usually for 5+ years at that point, under my supervision.

You cannot afford time off training for stupid injuries. Life's too short. Whatever training you are doing must, must, must leave you healthier than when you started it. You will not win Olympic gold medals this way, but you won't end up a cripple either. The path to sporting glory is littered with the shattered bodies and minds of the unlucky many who broke themselves on the way. Don't join them.

THE FIRST CLASS

STARTING AT THE BEGINNING

The purpose of the first class is to introduce you to to the historical source, *Gran Simulacro*; to get you doing something rapier-like; and to teach you how to train safely. That's all.

In the salle, my class begins with a short speech of welcome, and then we go look at The Book. My one deep secret fear is that one day, a student will come to one of my classes and come away thinking that I made it all up. The Book in this case is Ridolfo Capoferro's *Il Gran Simulacro dell'Arte e dell'Uso della Scherma* (The Great Representation of the Art and the Use of Fencing), which was first published in 1610. It is perhaps the most famous fencing treatise ever written, and in its time it went through many editions. For such a famous work, we know almost nothing about the author save that which he tells us himself: he was 52 at the time of writing and he came from Cagli, in Italy.

For modern practitioners, the two most useful translations are Tom Leoni's, published as *The Art and Practice of Fencing,* by Freelance Academy Press, and Jherek Swanger and William Wilson's free translation, which you can find here: https://guywindsor.net/blog/sources/ along with a scan of the original book.

We begin with a warm-up, which serves several functions. Firstly, it prepares you for the specific actions of the style, and secondly, it allows the instructor to see all the students move, which tells them a great deal about what they need to teach you about how to do various actions.

Warm-up Video
https://guywindsor.net/blog/rbc001

Notes

(Include information like: the dates of your practices, any actions that were particularly difficult, or felt particularly helpful, links to additional resources. Ideally you will have a complete record of your progress.)

The Guard Position

Now for the guard position. This will take some time to get perfect (in my case three years to "good", perfect is still some way off). Capoferro clearly describes every aspect of the guard position (see in particular Tables 67, 72 and 83). Combining this with the information in the illustrations (especially Plates 2-6), we may summarise the main points:

1. Stand with your heels together, your feet at right angles to each other, your right foot (if you're right-handed) pointing forwards,

2. drop your weight onto your left foot, bending the knee a little,

3. keep your weight on your left foot as you advance your right foot forwards as far as you can,

4. keep your back upright, and your head up, looking forwards,

5. hold an imaginary pint of beer in your right hand, and push a dwarf in the face with your left.

Check the placement of the weight by passing the front foot back, without moving anything else. An imaginary bowl of water on your head should not spill or fall. Imaginary whisky (a good single malt, of course) works even better.

Guard Position Video
https://guywindsor.net/blog/rbc002

Notes

The Lunge

Once you can get into the guard position, the next thing to learn is the lunge. This is one of the most important actions, and is often thought of as the defining feature of Italian rapier fencing. Capoferro calls it *l'incredibile accrescimento della botta lunga* ("the incredible increase of the long blow").

To start with, keep the lunge short and safe. It's a good idea to have a spotter handy to check the alignment of your front knee and foot. A mirror is also handy.

1. Begin in the guard position as defined in the previous drill.

2. Reach forwards with your right hand (if you're right-handed),

3. when your arm is straight, allow your shoulders to edge forwards, and step forwards with your front foot,

4. pushing yourself forwards with your back leg,

5. and throwing your left arm behind you in line with your shoulders and right arm.

6. To recover, grab an imaginary handle with your left hand, and pull yourself back to the guard position, leaving your arm extended.

7. Recover your arm.

Practise with your back foot remaining glued flat to the ground at first. When that is comfortable, notice that by turning on the ball of the back foot, you can push your hips a bit further forwards, thus extending your reach. Capoferro explicitly refers to this turn of the foot. Play with it a bit, then try to do it *during* the lunge, while your front foot is moving. The risk is that it tends to generate a turn in the hips, which can twist your front knee, so use a mirror or spotter until you can make the turn correctly.

Lunge Video
https://guywindsor.net/blog/rbc003

Notes

Stepping, Forwards and Backwards

Steps are the delivery system for the lunge; a step that leaves you unbalanced, or unable to lunge, is not useful.

Stepping forwards:
1. Stand on guard, with your weight on the ball of your left foot

2. Step your front foot forwards a few inches

3. Keeping your weight on your back foot, bring your back foot forwards the same distance as your front foot shifted.

Stepping backwards:
1. Stand on guard.

2. Ensure that your weight is on the balls of your feet, and that you are firmly controlling your centre of gravity.

3. Without moving your weight forwards at all, shift your weighted back foot a few inches back. Be careful to step on the ball.

4. Bring your front foot back the same distance that your back foot moved.

The steps should be neat, clean, brisk and precise.

Controlling Measure

The purpose of footwork is to control measure and deliver power. We will get on to power later, but for now, you need to be able to use your footwork to control the distance between yourself and your partner. For this we have a simple exercise:

Stepping Video
https://guywindsor.net/blog/rbc004

Controlling Measure
https://guywindsor.net/blog/rbc005

Notes

Footwork Summary

You now know how to stand on guard, lunge, and step forwards and backwards. These three things will form about 80% of your rapier fencing footwork. So take some time to play with them; combining steps and lunges until your form really suffers. Then stop, tidy yourself up, and start again.

Grounding

While we are on the subject of footwork, we should discuss the concept of grounding. This is critically important, and I cover it in some depth in *The Theory and Practice of Historical Martial Arts*. From page 270:

Every action has an equal and opposite reaction: when you hit the target, the target hits back. That energy has to go somewhere. If it is not carefully directed, it may very well go into shocking your joints. so it is necessary to establish a safe route for the kinetic energy coming back from the target. It either moves the weapon (not ideal, usually), or is routed down into the ground through the passive structure of your skeleton. This skill can be refined for decades, but I find that even beginners can generate major improvements if we simply create the position of the moment of impact (the lunge, for instance) and apply very gentle pressure in the reciprocal direction to the strike. The student can feel the place where it takes most effort to hold the position (the lead shoulder, for instance), and create a correction to the position that allows the same pressure to be absorbed with less effort. Then we can apply the pressure at the beginning of the movement and establish that the entire movement is properly grounded. (This is much easier with thrusts than cuts, obviously.) Ultimately, we are looking for a structure which does not need to change at all to route the energy: when we add the pressure, there is no need for any kind of muscular reaction, nor any increase in effort or tension.

This sort of practice leads to all sorts of gains in efficiency: the starting position, the movement, and the end position are all naturally grounded, and so all the muscular effort being made is directly applying force to the strike. Muscles that are not working to hold the position are available for generating power, so a deeply relaxed guard and a deeply relaxed movement allow for massive increases in power generation.

The critical thing is to *experience* the groundpath through your body. This is not just an academic idea, it's visceral.

Grounding
https://guywindsor.net/blog/rbc006

Notes

Holding the Sword

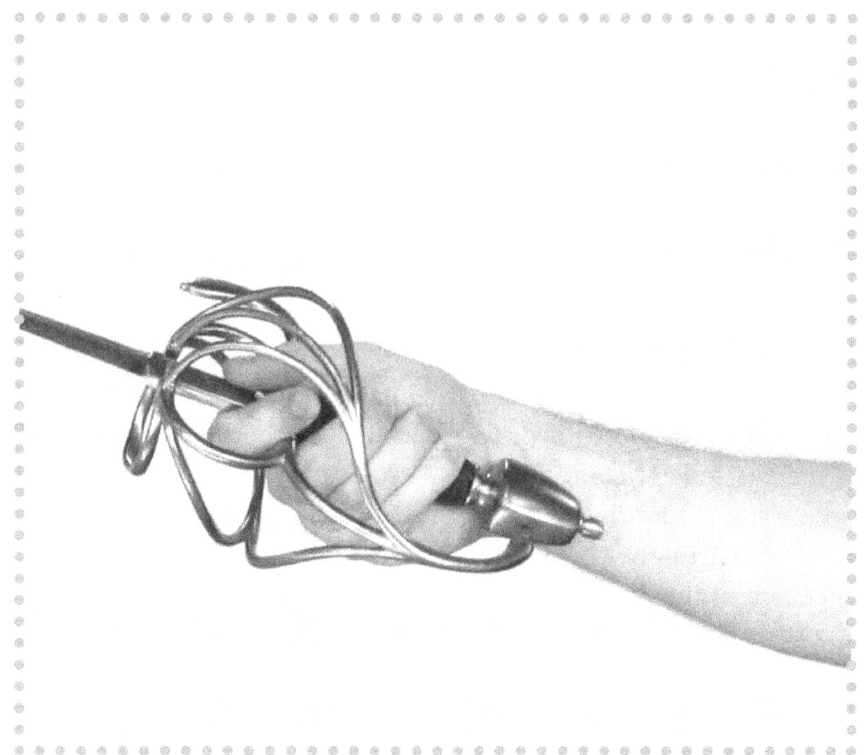

How you hold the sword is really important. A beginner will tend to grip it in a fist, and force the weapon through its motions with the muscles of the shoulder. Beginners' arms get tired quickly!

The optimum grip allows you to passively absorb the weight of the sword (or its tendency to fall), and take advantage of that natural motion. We hook the sword with one finger, and prop up the pommel on the base of the palm.

We call this the Ozzy Osbourne grip. Watch the video to see why.

Having learned to hold the sword, you should now practise all the footwork you can remember, with sword in hand.

Grip the Sword Video
https://guywindsor.net/blog/rbc007

Parts of the Sword

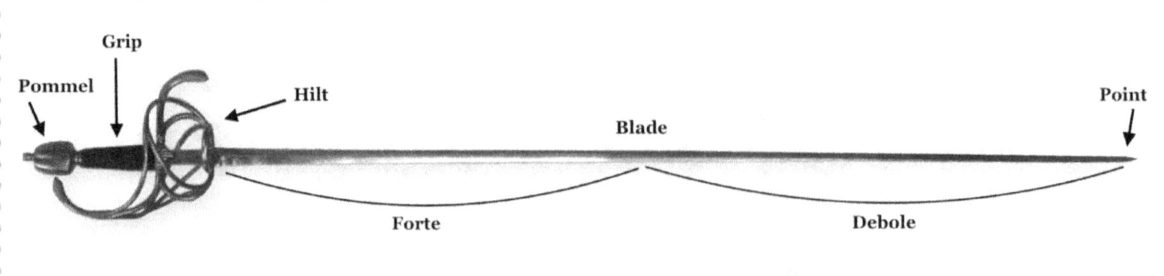

You need to know the following parts of the sword:

The blade: this has two edges and a point (Capoferro says). The edge that is held away from you (the one you would whittle with if it was a knife) is the true edge (***filo dritto***) the one towards you is the false edge (*filo falso*).

The half of the blade closest to the point is called the debole (weak), the one closer to the hilt is called the forte (strong).

The hilt is made up of the pommel, the grip, and the hilt (yes, really. Hilt means the whole blunt end of the sword, and the fancy swirly bit that protects your fingers. Sorry.)

Notes

The Four Guards

Capoferro shows us six guards of the sword and dagger, numbered (in Italian) prima, seconda, terza, quarta, quinta, and sesta (first, second, third, fourth, fifth, and sixth). He ascribes a letter to each one also, A-F, which is very useful because in each Platethe action normally began with both fencers in different guards, and each one is lettered with the guard they began in.

In the first section of the plates dealing with the sword alone he only refers to the first four of the six guards, prima to quarta, so we will start with those. All six illustrations show the guards held with the sword and dagger, so don't worry about the position of the left hand at this stage: holding a dagger can change it to a degree.

Prima is held above the head, in the position you would end up in having just drawn the sword.

Seconda is held about shoulder level, with the true edge of the sword turned out to the side away from you.

Terza is held about waist level, with the true edge turned down towards the floor.

Quarta is held with the sword turned to the inside.

Plate 2 shows quarta and prima:

Notes

Plate 3 shows seconda and sesta

And Plate 4 shows terza and quinta.

It's worth noting that Capoferro does not discuss blade orientation, nor does he treat the guards as highly specific fixed positions. Instead, he treats the position of the hand as the determining factor: above the shoulder is prima, about level with the shoulder is seconda, below the shoulder, sort of in the middle, is terza, and to the inside is quarta.

For practical purposes, especially in the early stages of training, we tend to be much more specific. Just file that thought away for later.

The Four Guards Video
https://guywindsor.net/blog/rbc008

Notes

The Sword: Forte and Debole

As Capoferro states in Chapter 3, paragraph 37:

> There are two parts to the sword: the forte and the debole. The forte begins from the hilt, extending as far as the middle of the blade; and the remainder is called the debole. The forte is for parrying, and the debole for striking.

This is really important, because:

If you always keep your forte in the way of the opponent's debole, you will never be hit. Let me say that again.

If you always keep your forte in the way of the opponent's debole, you will never be hit.

So we of course have about a million exercises for training this. Starting with Hunt the Debole:

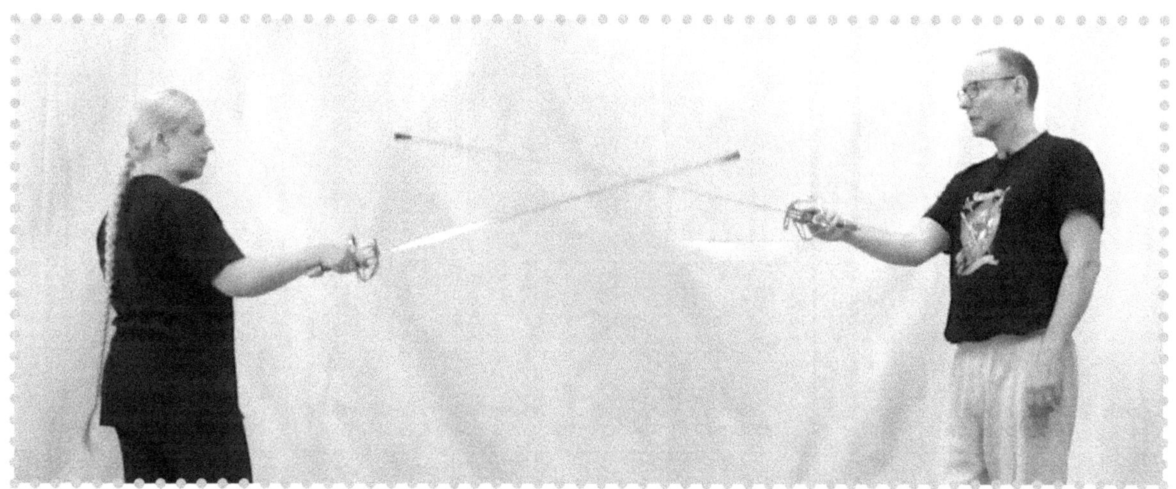

Hunt the Debole

This game is played to improve sword handling skills and endurance. Start with the blades engaged, and as one player acquires a dominant blade relationship, the other tries to prevent them and acquire dominance themselves. This is done with any combination of disengages and changes of line. This is normally done after footwork and before specific technical drills.

1. Start with your forte against your partner's debole. You could strike, they could not.

2. So they can either change the line, by moving their forte to your debole, pushing your debole out of the way, or they can take their sword point round under your forte, bringing it up on the other side, and find your debole with their forte.

3. This leaves you at a disadvantage; so you either "change the line" or "disengage".

The Italian term for the disengage is *"cavazione"*.

Hunt the Debole Video
https://guywindsor.net/blog/rbc009

Notes

Plate 7: Step by Step

I think it is really important that all students in my school understand that I am not making this stuff up. It comes from THE BOOK. So the first proper "technique" we will cover is the first illustrated strike in *Gran Simulacro*, which is shown on Plate 7.

However, we don't dive right in. It's really important that the logic behind every action is clear. So, we begin with a very unrealistic set-up: you approach your partner, and they just stand still.

Instructors' note: *At this stage, at least some of my colleagues will be horrified: we haven't covered utterly fundamental stuff like the guard positions with the sword, and various other things. This is because this is a four week course; most of those things will come next week. But I want every student present to have done at least one historically documented technique in their first class. Feel free to move things around and teach a simple parry-riposte here.*

1. You both put on masks, and your partner stands on guard, pointing their sword at your face.

2. You approach, with your sword on the right of theirs, putting your forte in the way of their debole; your hand is palm up.

3. When you are close enough, you gently extend your arm and lunge, hitting them lightly in the face.

4. Recover out of measure with two passes back, keeping your forte in the way of their debole the whole way.

Take turns doing this. The point at which you are close enough to strike with a single action (such as the lunge), you are *in measure*. Positioning your sword such that they can't strike you is called *stringering* (constraining), or "gaining the sword". We call this drill 'step one of Plate 7'.

The point is to make it clear how your sword position allows you to strike without being struck. It should also be obvious that no sane person will stand still and get hit like that. So, let's have you react to the approach.

1. As your partner approaches towards being in measure, watch for the moment that they step close enough to strike.

2. As they take that step, you must disengage, find their debole, and strike.

Take turns doing this, which we call 'step two of Plate 7'.

Plate 7, steps 1 and 2 Video
https://guywindsor.net/blog/rbc010

Notes

So now we have the circumstances described in the text of Plate 7: brace yourselves for the real thing!

THE PRESENT AND SUBSEQUENT FIGURES DEMONSTRATE DIVERSE MANNERS OF STRIKING ON THE OUTSIDE, ALWAYS

Presupposing A Stringering On The Inside And A Disengage Of The Point By Your Adversary In Order To Strike

By way of clarification of the following figures, I say that D having the figure marked C stringered on the inside, the same C disengages in order to give a thrust to the chest of figure D. D strikes them with a thrust in the left eye with a fixed foot or an increase of pace as the figure shows.

But yet I say that if C had been a shrewd person, when he disengaged he would have disengaged by way of a feint, with his body somewhat held back, and D approaching confidently in order to attack C, C would have parried the enemy's sword to the outside with the false or the true edge, giving him a mandritto to the face or an imbroccata to the chest, and in such a conclusion would retire into a low quarta.

(Sorry about the shouty CAPS: they're in the original.)

Notes

Let's leave aside what C would have done if he had been a clever person (that's coming in the next class) and focus on the illustrated action.

1. Approach your partner, stringering their sword.

2. As your partner disengages to strike, catch their debole as they do the disengage, turning your hand over (palm down). Aim your point at their left eye, and lunge. For safety's sake, your partner should leave out the lunge they were going to attack with.

If you've done everything right, it will look just like the plate, only (I hope) you will be training with clothes on. And masks. We call this 'step three of Plate 7'.

At the end of this first class we have covered the fundamental ideas of the art of the rapier, of historical swordsmanship, and of safe training. Not a bad start!

One final note: in our warm-up we didn't do any push-ups. Not one. We should fix that next time!

Notes

THE SECOND CLASS

TO STRIKE AND NOT BE STRUCK

The second class includes lots of revision from the first class. This doesn't make a lot of sense from a book perspective, so I'll just include references to the repeated material rather than writing it all out again.

Warm-up

This week's warm-up is closer to a normal class warm-up, and it includes the promised push-ups. It's a big jump from the previous warm-up, so feel free to work up to it slowly, or just repeat the last class's warm-up.

Footwork Revision

Memory is a skill, and must be trained like any other. At this stage you should do all the footwork stuff you remember. Do NOT check back to get reminders: recognition and recollection are two very different processes. We're working on recollection. Go through it for two solid minutes.

Done?

Notes

OK, now watch this:

And practice slowly and carefully. This will be our base for a while.

Now let's work on the lunge itself.

The Lunge, against pressure

In this exercise, your partner applies a gentle pressure, for you to establish your groundpath, and maintain it as you lunge.

As we saw in the previous class, the groundpath is the route that force travels between your hand and the ground. It should be a passive process; with every bone in the right place, the force just travels down them. In this exercise, your right arm is extended, and your partner gently presses on it, towards your shoulder. Your job is to direct that pressure into your back foot. Wherever you feel muscular tension is needed, that's where you should make a small postural correction.

Once you can feel the groundpath, you can think of the lunge as a taking that curved groundpath and snapping it into a straight line. For most students, this is quite straightforward. The hard part is maintaining the groundpath as you recover …

Notes

Now take up swords and review the grip. Familiarise yourself with the weapon by going through some footwork with the sword in hand, and then spend a few minutes on Hunt the Debole (see above).

The Cavazione

Having refreshed your memory of Hunt the Debole, we can look at one of its key components, the cavazione, or disengage. Try to make the cavazione as small as possible, using as little effort as possible, and immediately gain control of the opponent's debole.

The Cavazione Video
https://guywindsor.net/blog/rbc015

Having reviewed and deepened your understanding of the cavazione, return to the Hunt the Debole exercise and try to apply that understanding to the drill.

Having done that, we add footwork! No need to stand still, and no strikes yet, but play the Hunt the Debole game using your feet to get you out of trouble if needed. Masks on, just in case.

Hunt the Debole, controlling measure Video
https://guywindsor.net/blog/rbc016

Having practised that, now revise Plate 7, steps 1-3.

Notes

Introducing Choice

It is very important that students are involved in the process of their own training. In class I set this up at the very beginning, by giving them a choice regarding what to cover next in their first or second class. We can either complete the plays of Plate 7, or start Plate 16. I would advise the latter, but it's a free choice. It's impossible to simulate this in a book while making sure you cover everything (those "choose your own adventure" books (if you can remember that far back) provide a model, but you don't get taken through every scene that way). If you want to skip along to the completion of Plate 7, be my guest.

It's useful to remember that fencing masters were usually hired professionals, and socially inferior to their clients. Salvatore Fabris taught Christian IV, King of Denmark. I don't think Fabris barked orders at His Majesty, do you?

Beginning Plate 16

Plate 16 begins with "C stretto to the outside of D..." in other words, your partner is in quarta, you approach to stringer on the outside, they attack by disengage, you parry and riposte in a single tempo in quarta, striking them under the right ear. It is just like Plate 7, only you enter on the other side.

Notes

Plate 16 steps 1-3 Video
https://guywindsor.net/blog/rbc017

Teaching note: Towards the end of the class, make time to let students practise freely; whatever they feel they need to work on. Give them two solid minutes without any interference from you at all, and then inform them that they have just demonstrated that they can practise without you for a couple of minutes… and so ought to be doing that every single day. No excuses now!

Breadth v. Depth

Learning new things is fun, and broadens our horizons. Studying to become expert in the things we are already familiar with is much harder, but generates much greater rewards. In every class, we always distinguish between breadth and depth. Imagine your fencing repertoire as a pyramid. It has to be taller than your opponent's pyramid to reliably win. Every new thing is a brick on the bottom layer of the pyramid. The pyramid must reach a certain height before it's actually useful. The broader the base, the higher you can build. Adding breadth adds to our base, building on that by developing skills adds to the height.

You need both, but depth beats breadth every time.

Notice how little new material is introduced on the second class; in the first class, *everything* is unfamiliar. Now that we have laid that base, we need to reinforce it, and from here on, *most* classes will be mostly revision, gradually building that pyramid higher and higher on its broad stable base.

Finish the class by going over plates 7 and 16 again.

THE THIRD CLASS

INTRODUCING THE FEINT

The class begins with a warm up. It is a good idea by this stage if you are able to warm yourself up without being led - but feel free to use the warm-up videos if you like.
Now run through the footwork that you know, some grounding, Hunt the Debole, and steps 1-3 of plates 7 and 16.
Take your time …

The Parry Riposte in Two Tempi

To complete Plate 7 you will need to know the parry riposte in two tempi, on both sides, against a simple attack, and the feint with body held back.

Let's start with the parry riposte in two tempi by setting up Plate 7 as before, but at step 3 instead of attacking on the cavazione (or, as Capoferro describes it, parrying and striking in a single motion), parry, turning your hand to seconda and meeting their debole with your forte, then riposte.

You can do this on the other side by setting up Plate 16, and as your partner attacks by disengage, parry by turning your hand to quarta meeting their debole with your forte, and riposte.

Parry riposte in two tempi Video
https://guywindsor.net/blog/rbc018

Notes

Plate 7, Complete

'Step four of Plateseven' is the counter to the play illustrated above on Plate 7 (which you know as step 3 of that drill). As 'D' approaches and stringers you, you feint, drawing your opponent into that action, onto your prepared defence, in this case a parry followed by a riposte.

When executing the feint, keep your body back, but disengage and extend your arm to make it look like you are attacking. As your partner attacks, parry and riposte as in the previous exercise.

1. Stand on guard in *terza*

2. partner stringers on the inside in *quarta*

3. disengage and feint in *seconda*, keeping your body back

4. partner falls for the feint, and turning their hand to *seconda*, attacks

5. as they do so, turn your hand to *prima*, collecting their sword on your true edge, and thrust them in the chest.

6. recover keeping control of their sword.

You may also parry with the false edge, and riposte with a cut to the head.

1. Stand on guard in *terza*

2. partner stringers on the inside in *quarta*

3. disengage and feint in *seconda*, keeping your body back

4. partner falls for the feint, and turning their hand to *seconda*, attacks

5. as your partner attacks in *seconda*, turn your hand to *terza* and strike their sword up and out with a *falso manco*,

6. and let your blade drop down in the same line as it went up, creating a natural *mandritto ordinario* to their head.

7. recover keeping control of their sword.

Once that is comfortable, practise the whole of Plate 7, step by step, with both versions of step four.

Notes

Plate 7 complete Video
https://guywindsor.net/blog/rbc019

Now that we have Plate 7 complete, introducing three new skills all at once (feinting, cutting, parrying and riposting in two tempi) give yourself time to consolidate. Spend some time doing some solo practice (with or without the sword), and then play a little Hunt the Debole (with or without footwork). Finally, from memory, walk through Plate 7 again, step by step.

THE FOURTH CLASS

CUTS AND COUNTERDISENGAGES

This class steps things up a level, beginning with the warm-up, where after the usual joint mobility exercises, we introduce this breathing exercise:

Breathing exercise Video
https://guywindsor.net/blog/rbc020

Notes

This video is extracted from my online course Fundamentals: Breathing. If you don't already have a breathing practice, I recommend you try the course, or read the relevant chapter in *The Theory and Practice of Historical Martial Arts.*

Once you have done that, go through your footwork drills, then take up the swords and revise:

* The four guards, solo
* Hunt the Debole
* Plate 7, steps 1-3, 4
* Plate 16, steps 1-3

Got that? Now let's complete Plate 16.

Notes

Plate 16, Complete

Set up Plate 16 again, with your partner stringering. This time, as you disengage, use the momentum of the disengage to beat your partner's sword away, cutting down through their blade diagonally, and finishing with your point in line with their chest. Then thrust to their chest.

The video goes into some depth regarding the mechanics of the beat. Your objective is to create a tempo in which you can safely strike. In short, you need to make the beat in the optimal line against your partner's blade to beat it aside. You do this by cutting across their groundpath, through the flat of their blade. Use the smallest motion that will get the job done.

Plate 16 complete Video
https://guywindsor.net/blog/rbc021

Notes

Cuts

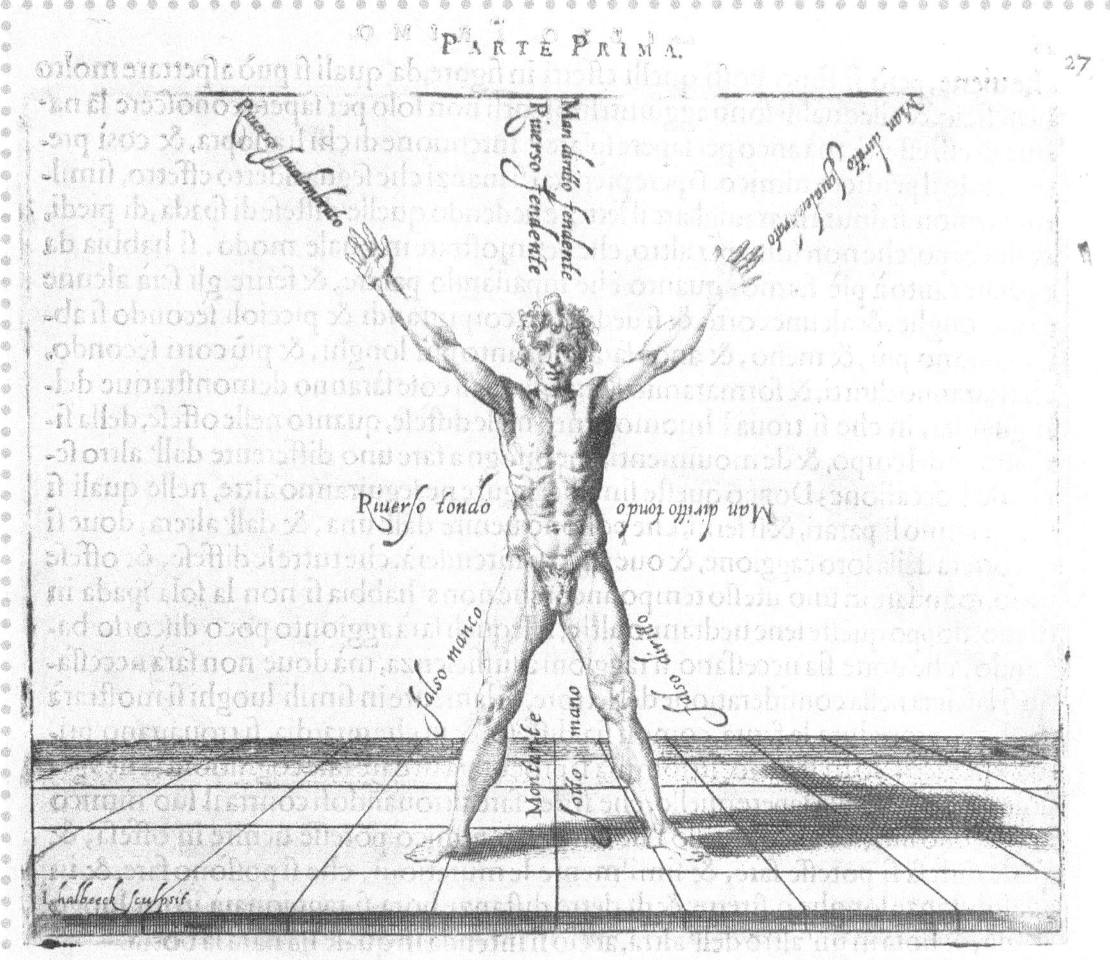

Completing Plate 7 introduced the idea of cuts, which we developed in step four of Plate 16 (the beat attack). We should take some time to make them more natural and comfortable, which will improve your execution of those two plays, as well as adding this essential element to your repertoire.

The cuts are named: *mandritto* (or *dritto*) means forehand; *riverso* (or *roverso*) means backhand. *Fendente* is straight down, *tondo* is across, *squalembro* is diagonally down, and the rising blows are called *falso manco* (backhand) and *falso dritto* (forehand).

A whirling blow from the wrist is a *stramazzone*. This cutting diagram comes from Salvatore Fabris' *Sienza e Pratica d'Arme* from 1606. Capoferro doesn't include one, but he does seem to use the same terminology.

Cuts Video
https://guywindsor.net/blog/rbc022

Notes

Plate 15: Contracavazione

So far, in plates 7 and 16, the person stringered always responds to the stringering with a disengage (followed by an attack, a feint, or a beat), and the person stringering responds to the disengage with parry-riposte in a single tempo. There are, of course, many alternatives, such as this one from Plate 15: the contracavazione, the counterdisengage.

One of the great advantages of introducing games like Hunt the Debole so early in your training is that now I barely need to discuss the contracavazione, because you have already done them *many times*. You just didn't know they were a thing.

Simply put: when you stringer, as your partner disengages, do a disengage of your own. This should return your blades to the previous relationship, with you in control of theirs. Use that tempo to strike.

Set this up as a variation on Plate 7, stringering on the inside, and on Plate 16, stringering on the outside.

As you can imagine, your attack by contracavazione can be countered by everything that the attack by cavazione has been countered by. Including, wait for it, your partner doing another disengage! This is called a redisengage, or ricavazione.

Contracavazione Video
https://guywindsor.net/blog/rbc023

At this stage, if not before, I would ask the class to choose breadth or depth. If breadth, go on to the next action, the scannatura. If depth, go back and work on making plates 7 and 16 better, through blocked practice and play.

Notes

Plate 13: The Scannatura

The scannatura, the 'butchering', is an alternative response to the attack by disengage onto your inside line. So, you stringer on the outside, your partner attacks by disengage onto your inside line, and you drop your point over theirs, beat their sword to the outside, then pass in, grabbing their hilt with your left hand.

Plate 13 the Scannatura Video
https://guywindsor.net/blog/rbc024

Once that is nice and comfortable, review the plates that you know, in order, and spend the rest of the class time working on the ones you find most difficult.

Notes

CONCLUSION

Now that you have completed this four-session course, you have covered all the major elements of rapier fencing except for avoidances and using off-hand weapons (such as the dagger or the cloak).

By themselves, Plate 7 and 16 give you:

- Stringering on both sides
- Attack by disengage on both sides
- Parry-riposte in one tempo
- Parry-riposte in two tempi
- Feint
- Beat attack
- Cuts

And we have added the contracavazione and the scannatura.

That is a very broad and stable base upon which to build your rapier skill. The question now is "what next?"

In short, next you develop your knowledge into skill, by getting better at executing the actions you have learned, and add to your knowledge by learning new things.

I hope you have found this course accessible and interesting, and this new workbook format to be really helpful. The obvious next step is to get Part 2 of this workbook series:

Rapier part Two: Completing the Basics
https://guywindsor.net/blog/rbc200

If 'proper' books are your thing, then you should probably get the Duellist's Companion.

The Duellist's Companion
https://guywindsor.net/blog/rbctdc

If you prefer video instruction, then The Essential Rapier Course (from which many of the videos in this workbook came) might suit you better.

You can use this link to get 50% off the regular price for the Essential Rapier Course:

Rapier Course Discount
https://guywindsor.net/blog/RBC2018

There are of course many other instructors out there whose approach you may enjoy and benefit from, so don't feel obliged to limit yourself to just mine.

QUICK QUIZ

As a quick test of how much you have picked up from this course, try answering these questions without looking anything up.

1. what is the debole?

2. when did Capoferro publish his book?

3. name the four guards that you know so far

4. what is a 'stringering'?

5. what is a cavazione, and how is it done?

6. what is a tempo?

7. what is the difference between a parry-riposte in a single tempo, and a parry riposte done in two tempi?

8. what is a feint?

9. what is a beat?

10. what is a *falso manco*? Can you parry with one?

How did you do? I've posted my answers on this page of my website:

https://guywindsor.net/blog/rapierbcwelcome

THE RAPIER

Part 2: Completing the Basics

— Workbook —

Guy Windsor

Published by Spada Press

© Guy Windsor and Spada Press 2018

ISBN: 978-952-7157-46-6 R2.1 Right-Handers

ISBN: 978-952-7157-47-3 R2.2 Left-Handers

This book belongs to:

…………………………………………………………………………………………………

Date begun: …………………………..

Date completed: …………………………

TABLE OF CONTENTS

INTRODUCTION

Creating a working syllabus is *hard*. Where do you start? What comes next? How do you know when you're ready to move on to the next thing? I find it helps to remember that there is no one correct answer, because the optimum structure for the syllabus depends on its goals, and the specific aptitudes and experience of the student.

The goal of this workbook is to add to the core actions you learned in the previous workbook (Rapier Part One: Beginners), covering all of the types of action we see in Capoferro. We will look at adding depth of skill in the next workbook; this one is all about broadening your base. We will therefore cover:

- Plate 8: voiding the front leg

- Plate 9: passing to attack (off-hand forwards)

- Plate 10: dealing with cuts to the head

- Plate 11: voiding low, and acting in *contratempo*

- Plate 17: voiding with the front foot

- Plate 18: passing to attack (off-hand back)

- Plate 19: voiding with the waist

- Capoferro's three tempi (half, full, and one-and-a-half)

- Changing direction

That is a lot of material, and hard to remember, so we will follow the structure of the Rapier Footwork Form; by the end of this book you will have a series of actions clearly stuck in your head, which will act as an aide-memoire for all the plates that you know (including everything in the previous book: plates 7, 13 and 16). That way, by running through the Form at the beginning of every training session, you will cover every major action in the system, and be reminded of the areas where you are strongest, and those that need most work.

I have also included some essential repetition from the previous book, notably the discussion on safety, and advice on how to use the book, because I know from experience that *some* readers will ignore "you need to read part one first", and those things *must* be read before training.

Some people just want to learn how to sword fight. Others want to learn how to do the academic research side of historical swordsmanship. And some want to do both. These workbooks are obviously directed towards the "just teach me to sword fight" crowd, but I encourage all my students (and that includes you!) to at least be familiar with the primary source for your art, in this case, *Gran Simulacro*. These workbooks will not cover *every* play from *every* plate, so in this book I will be encouraging you to fill in the gaps, and come up with your own interpretation of the plates we skip over. You don't have to do it, of course – you don't have to do anything I tell you, I'm not your mother. But I recommend it highly, and look forward with keen anticipation to you sending me links to go see your work…

What is Form?

Before teaching you the Rapier Footwork Form (as we call it), we should first discuss what form is, and what it is for. Fundamentally, form is the mechanism we use for creating a narrative of the system within the students' brains. You can think of a form as a string of pearls. In the beginning, each pearl is just one technique or action. It's a tiny little seed pearl. But with practise, and a broadening understanding of the Art, each pearl becomes the locus for other concepts and actions to be stored. A single action acts as a trigger for a cascade of related actions. Form is therefore a set of chapter headings, under which you can store everything you ever learn about swordsmanship with the rapier; and once you have filled out each chapter, you have an index to your entire knowledge base.

I cannot state this too strongly: the Form is just the beginning. It is not the be-all and end-all. When you write your own chapters, it becomes The Book of your rapier knowledge and skill. Once that is established you can simply run through the Form at any time and identify the weakest link. Start working on that link, using the "attached" training material, then re-run the Form to see whether what you have been working on is still the weakest link. The Form is therefore a diagnostic tool, an aide-memoire, a mechanics exercise or a guide to the system; in fact, it is the core of your practice. This workbook is about writing those chapter headings, and then filling in those chapters.

The major pitfall of this approach is that the organisation of the material in the Form has more to do with training space constraints and what felt good when designing it ("where do I want to go from here?") than it does with any overtly logical structure. It does not, for example, follow the order of the plates in *Gran Simulacro*. Nor is it arranged according to difficulty. You may find yourself wanting to re-arrange things. That's fine: the structure is (as with all forms) at least partly arbitrary. You only need to have this canonically correct if you are following my school's syllabus and intending to grade within it. Otherwise, take this and make it your own!

When I was a kid, I spent some time casting little lead soldiers. It was magic: you heat up the lead in a pan until it melts, pour it into the mould and wait for it to cool down, and out comes a cavalry officer, rifleman or whatever. We then had to trim off the inevitable little leaks and the rather large riser (the extra bit where you pour the metal in, called a "sprue" in the US). Then the figures were ready for painting. You can think of the Form in a similar way. The actions of the person doing the Form are moulded by the actions of the (imaginary or real) opponents, as well as by the overall training goals. As with the casting process, there are artefacts to be taken into account: little bits of metal that don't really belong, or some turns or steps that you wouldn't normally use but are necessary to keep the Form in the right shape.

So long as you know what the Art should look like and what the applications are, or what a Royal Horse Guards trooper from 1815 is supposed to look like, the Form is useful. As soon as the mould (your understanding of which actions do what) gets sloppy, the Form becomes a shapeless, pointless mess.

So here is a rule to be followed whenever you think about any kind of Form:

Application first, Form second.

We do this in class. When teaching the Form to students, we absolutely always do pair-drill (or handling drill) first, then the same actions solo, and then we add it to the Form. We never, ever, have students practising actions that they don't know at least one application for, and we distinguish very clearly between a play or technique and a handling drill or skill-development exercise.

I am still assuming the following things:

1. You have worked through Part One: Beginners. Seriously, do that before trying any of this

2. you are physically and mentally healthy enough to train

3. you want to actually practise with the sword

4. you want to practise in a historically authentic style

5. you have at least one friend to train with

6. you have some basic equipment: a training sword and a mask per person, a pen and a smartphone (or other device for watching internet videos)

7. you rightly believe that the rapier is the most elegant, most sophisticated, perfect sword (or at least are willing to believe it long enough to read the book).

The Rapier Footwork Form

This form was developed over many months in class, with input from at least a dozen different people, most notably Tanda Tuovinen, Janne Högdahl, Zoë Chandler, Henry Vilhunen, Henri Vesala, in addition to myself. It is divided into two parts, with a turn in between so that it will fit across the width of our Helsinki Salle. It goes like this:

Part One:
1. Step, step, lunge, recover with two passes backwards, such as we do in Plate 7 and Plate 16. We covered this already in the first workbook

2. Step, slip the leg. This is from Plate 8

3. Step back, extension; step back, strike with the fixed foot; step back, lunge with two passes forwards. These are based on Capoferro's half tempo, full tempo, and tempo and a half

4. Step forwards, void with the right foot (*scanso del pie dritto*). This is from Plate 17. Turn to face the other way.

Part Two:

1. Step, pass left ducking low, recover forwards. This is from Plate 11

2. Step, pass forwards, recover forwards. This is the *Scannatura* from Plate 13. We covered this already in the first workbook

3. Step, pass forwards, recover backwards. This is from Plate 18

4. Step, void with the waist (*scanso della vita*). This is from Plate 19.

As we go through the Form in the classes, I will expand on each step. For example, when we cover Plate 8, in which your opponent cuts at your leg and you slip the leg out of the way, we will also complete that plate, adding in the opponent's alternative to the cut to the leg, which is a cut to the head. We will then go and cover Plate 10, which has your counter to the cut to the head. All of that material will be mentally stored under the heading "Plate 8", which is referred to in the second step of the Form.

You can check out the whole form here:

The Footwork Form
https://guywindsor.net/blog/rbc201

A Note to Left-Handers

As I said in Part One: if you are left-handed:

For solo training, just reverse all left-right instructions.

For pair drills with a fellow lefty, reverse all left-right instructions, but keep inside and outside instructions the same.

For pair drills with a right hander (curse them), reverse your left-right instructions, but also reverse inside/outside instructions too. I'll give some examples as they arise in the book.

Please note also that I have produced two versions of this book; if you're left-handed, you'll find writing up notes much easier in the version of the book laid out for left-handers. If you've bought the wrong one by accident, email me and I'll send you the print file for the other version.

Equipment

For this level you will still need only a training rapier and a fencing mask. If you have more equipment feel free to use it, but in keeping with the 'funnel' idea, I like to keep requirements for basic training to a minimum.

Using this Workbook

Work through the book, annotating as you go, and you will finish it with a complete basic understanding of Capoferro's rapier system, in theory and in practice.

I have divided the book up into four classes of about 90 minutes each. You may well find that without a live instructor there you may need more time to go through the material. It is better to slow down and really get to grips with the material you are working on, than to try to cram too much material into the allotted time. Some folk work in 30-minute blocks, some in three hours; it's impossible to pick a division that works for everyone. Please treat the division into classes as a suggestion, not a rule!

It is very important that you clearly distinguish between blocked practice and play. In blocked practice you will set up a drill choreographically, and practise it as accurately as you can. This is an essential starting point – it teaches you *what to practise*. By itself though, it isn't really practice at all. For serious skill development we have many approaches, the most important of which is play. I introduce play in the very first class, and you will be learning how to play usefully throughout this course. Just be advised that "play" does not equal "do what the hell you like". Every game has rules, and to use the games effectively, you must pay attention to those rules and play within them. For a detailed breakdown of how to develop skill, there's a whole chapter on it in *The Theory and Practice of Historical Martial Arts*, and I plan to cover it in the next instalment of this series.

Safety

When training with weapons you hold your partner's life in your hands. This is a sacred trust and must not be abused.

Disclaimer: I accept no responsibility of any kind for injuries you sustain while you are not under my direct personal supervision. During this course you will be taught how to create safe training drills, and I am certain that if you follow the instructions there is a very low likelihood of injury. But if I am not there in person to create and sustain a safe training environment, I cannot be held responsible for any accidents that may occur.

Principles

The basic principles of safe training are:

1. Respect: for the Art, your training partners, the weapons, and yourself.

2. Caution: assume everything is dangerous unless you have reason to believe otherwise.

3. Know your limits. Just because it's safe for somebody else, does not necessarily mean it's safe for you. Never train or fence when you are tired, angry, or in any state of mind or body that makes accidents and injuries more likely.

You cannot afford time off training for stupid injuries. Life's too short. Whatever training you are doing must, must, must leave you healthier than you started it. You will not win Olympic gold medals this way, but you won't end up a cripple either. The path to sporting glory is littered with the shattered bodies and minds of the unlucky many who broke themselves on the way. Don't join them.

THE FIFTH CLASS

RETREAT BUT NO SURRENDER

This class will cover the first two steps of the Footwork Form, which are:

1. Step, step, lunge, recover with two passes backwards. (Such as you did in Plate 7 and 16)

2. Step, slip the leg, from Plate 8

We will also look at a defence against the cut.

Begin with a warm-up, play Hunt the Debole (standing still and with movement), and walk through Plates 7 and 16. Pay particular attention to the cuts, and revise them if you feel they are not firmly in memory.

When that's done, take the stringerer's footwork from both 7 and 16, and practise it on its own: step, step, lunge, recover with two passes. You can do this with or without the sword. If you use the sword, be careful that your blade is in exactly the right place relative to your imaginary opponent's.

Great, that's step 1 of the Form done. Now let's have a look at Plate 8.

Notes

Plate 8: Slip the Leg

This plate is explicitly intended to demonstrate an error in theory on the part of the opponent (figure C): "how much measure is lost by attacking the legs". As they cut at your front leg, you slip it and strike. As usual, Capoferro provides an alternative action on the part of the opponent: they could have attacked with "a riverso to the face followed by a mandritto fendente to the head, and thus they would have been safer". By now you are probably able to handle a four-step drill without too much difficulty, so I won't break it down into steps 1-3 followed by step 4, but feel free to do so if you find any part of steps 1-3 sticky.

1. Stringer your partner on the inside, as in Plate 7

2. As you do so, they disengage and cut at your leg.

3. As they do that, slip your leg, and thrust to the face (mask), or cut to the arm as you see in the plate.

4. or, as you stringer, your partner disengages and cuts a riverso fendente to your face, immediately followed by a cut to the head.

Plate 8: Slip the leg
https://guywindsor.net/blog/rbc202

The Footwork Form, Steps One and Two

Go through the stringerer's action of plate 8 on your own, with or without the sword. You step into measure, and as your imaginary opponent strikes your leg, slip it behind you while striking. If that's not clear, go back to the pair drill. If it is, then add it to step one. The Form now looks like this:

1. Step, step, lunge, recover with two passes backwards.

2. Step, slip the leg.

Practice that a few times until it's stable.

We will learn to defend against that cut to the face as shown on Plate 10 shortly, but first let's take a moment to look at passing footwork.

Notes

Passing Footwork

In Plate 13 (the *scannatura*) you used a pass forwards with the back foot to bring your off-hand forwards to grip your partner's hilt. Now in Plate 8, you have effectively passed back with your front foot, leaving your sword-hand forwards to strike. You have also recovered from the lunge with two passes, keeping your sword forwards, many times by now.

In essence, there are two kinds of passes: those that turn the torso, bringing the other side forwards (e.g. *scannatura*); and those that keep the torso in its original alignment (e.g. slip the front leg).

An easy way to get the feel of this is to walk across the room, normally. Notice what your hands do.

The right hand goes forwards when the left foot goes, and vice versa. This is what keeps your body square on.

Now try walking but deliberately make your right hand track your right foot.

Feels weird? It is. Your hips and shoulders now turn with every step.

Generally speaking, when rapier fencing we use the turning pass to enter in to grip the opponent's sword, and the ordinary pass to quickly gain measure or retreat.

It is a good idea to practise these passes on their own, to get a clear feel for the distinction.

Passing
https://guywindsor.net/blog/rbc203

Notes

Plate 10: Defending Against the Cut

Plate 10 teaches us what to do when somebody responds to our stringering on the inside by disengaging and cutting at our face. Basically, you stick your sword in the way, and into them, moving aggressively forwards. I usually teach this plate separated out into parts 1-3 and then 4 (what C should have done instead of the cut), because step 4 is a little more complicated than an alternative attack (such as the one we saw on Plate 8). It will follow the same basic pattern as Plate 7, with a disengage to feint. But let's not get ahead of ourselves:

1. Stringer on the inside, as in Plate 7

2. Your partner disengages to cut the face, exactly as in step 4 of Plate 8

3. As they do so, keep your hand in quarta, lifting it and stepping in aggressively with the front foot. You catch their cut on your hilt, while stabbing them in the chest.

Amongst friends, try this deliberately missing their chest, so you can lunge faster and deeper. If you are going to strike the proper target, you'll have to ease off on the lunge, because your sword won't go through their chest (or it had certainly better not!).

Plate 10, steps 1-3
https://guywindsor.net/blog/rbc204

Notes

Plate 10, Complete

Capoferro tells us that if C had been a clever person they would have disengaged by way of a feint with the body held back (sounds a lot like Plate 7, right?)

In the Swanger and Wilson translation, the instruction reads:

> However, I say that if C, instead of turning the riverso, had drawn back his sword while retiring back somewhat, and lifted his sword in an oblique line so that its point faced toward the adversary's left side, and D had wanted to enter in quarta, C, parrying with a mezzo mandritto, would have given him a riverso to the face or a thrust to the chest.

I do this by disengaging and lifting my point up to my right, while bringing my front foot back a few inches. This is a nice big invitation to my opponent, who enters in quarta; I then parry their sword down with the half-mandritto (which means the point stays in the centre, and does not drop any further), then strike.

Plate 10, Complete
https://guywindsor.net/blog/rbc205

5

Notes

THE SIXTH CLASS

GET OUT OF THE WAY

In this class we will look at Capoferro's "three tempi" in some depth, and then move on to the next step of the Footwork Form, which introduces avoidances.

Begin as usual with a warm-up, revise your footwork, and run through the first two steps of the Footwork Form. Make sure that's all comfortable, before moving on.

Extension, Lean, and Lunge

You already know how to strike with a lunge, and how to strike with a pass forwards (Plate 13) and backwards (plate 8). It is also possible to strike by just extending your arm (as in the beginning of the lunge), and by doing an action that is basically lunging without moving the front foot – you just push your weight onto it, bending the front knee. We call this the 'lean'. You need to be able to clearly distinguish those three actions before we can move on to Capoferro's 'three tempi'.

Extension, Lean and Lunge, solo
https://guywindsor.net/blog/rbc206

The Three Tempi

Be warned: I'm going to go full-on academic geek. This is because I want you to see where this material is coming from, and to understand the changes we are making from a strict by-the-book interpretation to fit our training goals. If you just want to get on with hitting things, that's fine, skip ahead. But don't blame me if your art lacks a certain depth later on.

Measure and Tempo

You will have noticed that some fencing actions are longer than others, and no doubt have wondered how that affects their use. It should be obvious that in defence you should always use a shorter action than your opponent; if your opponent lunges, and you must also lunge to defend yourself, you would have to be much faster than them to make it work. So it is useful to have a way of defining the lengths of certain key actions. Capoferro confines himself to discussing the different lengths of only three actions: the extension of the sword arm; the strike with the lean; and the lunge. In his terminology, they require respectively a half tempo, a full tempo, and a tempo and a half, to execute.

The term "tempo" is used frequently in *Gran Simulacro* and many other fencing texts, and it can apply to a range of concepts. In essence, a tempo is a movement, or a period of stillness, and an opportunity to strike. Briefly put, if my opponent moves, there is a chance to strike; if they stay still, there is another chance to strike; as I move to strike, or stand still, there is a tempo in which I may be struck.

This only occurs, of course, when the distance between you and your opponent is such that one or other, or both, are close enough to hit each other in a single action (or tempo).

Imagine you and your opponent are facing each other, a long way apart. Your opponent stands still, while you approach. For the sake of clarity, we will assume that you have equal reaches. The longest single attack is actually the pass, but it is rarely used as a direct attack, as it is too obvious and slow. So, the instant you step into range for your lunge, either you or your opponent can strike with the lunge. Your last step is in fact a tempo, in which you may be struck.

This last step carries you into what Capoferro calls *la misura stretta del piedi accresciuto*, the narrow measure of the increased foot (because with an increase of the front foot, i.e. a step, you can strike). This is, in his system, the first, or longest *misura stretta*. *Misura stretta* literally means narrow, closed or tight measure, and refers to the distances in which you can strike with a single action. This longest *misura stretta* is also known as *misura larga*, or wide measure. (Other rapier systems use the terms differently; normally, wide measure is lunging distance, and narrow measure includes all distances in which you can strike without taking a step. Capoferro is unique in calling wide measure the longest of the narrow measures. This is only important when comparing Capoferro's method to other systems; just remember that he is using the term *misura stretta* more comprehensively than others.)

Now, if you take one more step from lunging measure (*misura larga)*, you should be able to strike your opponent with just the lean. This is *la misura stretta di pie fermo*, the narrow measure of the fixed foot (because your front foot doesn't move when you strike).

Note: other masters of this period, such as Giganti, use the term 'pie fermo' to refer to the lunge. It's a question of which foot is fixed. In the lunge, the back foot doesn't move, which is what

Giganti is referring to. This distinguishes the lunge from the pass. Capoferro is distinguishing this leaning strike by referring to the front *foot being fixed, which distinguishes the lean from the lunge.*

This is a great example of how different masters can use the same terminology to mean different things. Bear this in mind when you start broadening your reading into other sources.

Lastly, if you edge a little closer, you can strike by simply extending your arm; this is *la misura stretta del braccio dritto*, the narrow measure of the right arm. (Left-handers, you would be in *la misura stretta del braccio sinistro*.)

It is clear then that the closer you are, the shorter your movement needs to be, so the less time it takes: distance and time are therefore, in fencing, co-dependent.

Capoferro goes on to explain (in Table 48, 112 and 113) when and where each action should be used: in essence, your principal attacking action is the lunge: few opponents will let you get any closer before trying to hit you. However, if your opponent lunges at you, they are crossing the distance between you, so you need only strike with the lean. If they come in more vigorously, you may step back and stab them in the arm. In this case, you are striking in the narrow measure of the right arm.

Capoferro describes (in Table 106) three main situations in which you will get into fighting distance: when your opponent is still and you move; when you are still and they move, and when you both move. The term tempo refers to any single movement (however long, and at whatever speed), and any single moment of stillness (however long). It also refers to the opportune moment in which a successful strike may be made. Tempo of course only applies when you are in measure, or entering into measure. Lastly, tempo can be qualified, and used to describe the timing of certain actions relative to an opponent (Capoferro defines these terms in Explanations, 3).

Let's say I am standing still, and my opponent approaches. The step that brings them in reach of my lunge is a tempo, in that it is a movement on their part done in measure; it is also a tempo in that it is a moment in which I can strike them, in this case with a lunge.

For the sake of this explanation, I do nothing. If they then stand still, the period in which they are standing still, yet are in range, is another tempo in which I can strike them. So I lunge at them. During my lunge, they must defend themselves, and that defence has to happen before my lunge finishes, or they're dead. So my lunge is a movement (i.e. a tempo) and a moment in which they must act (i.e. a tempo). If they have done nothing, I hit them in my first action, hence, in primo tempo.

If they choose to strike me by closing the line of my attack, and hit me with a lean as I come forward, by striking me with a shorter tempo (movement) and measure (the distance is narrower because we are both coming forward), they are said to strike in *contra tempo* (counter time: refer to Explanations 3). If they get rid of my blade and hit me in the same single movement, they may be said to strike in a single tempo, or parry and strike in the same tempo.

They could choose to beat my blade aside with a cut (which is a movement, and therefore a tempo), then hit me with a second movement (hence a second tempo). So they defend themselves in *due tempi*; with two tempos, or in double time. Recall Plate 7: the one who stringers 'parries and ripostes in one single motion'; the one stringered can, if they disengage with a feint, parry and riposte in two motions.

Or they may step back a little and stab me in the arm as I come forward: because this action

Notes

is so short, it is called a half-tempo, or *mezzo tempo*.

It's about time that you were able to set up basic drills from simple written instructions – if you think about it, that's the heart of interpreting historical sources. So I won't provide a video for these: I want you to create these drills just from the page.

Narrowest measure:
1. Stand on guard in terza.

2. Partner enters into wide measure, stringering your sword on the inside as above.

3. Partner fully extends and lunges.

4. As they do so, step back a little (as in the stepping back exercise) and thrust to their forearm.

Narrow measure of the fixed foot:
1. Partner stands on guard in terza.

2. Enter into wide measure, stringering your partner on the inside as above.

3. Close in a little to the narrow measure of the fixed foot as you stringer, extend your arm, and lean in to strike.

4. Recover, maintaining opposition.

Pay careful attention to your distance: too close and you don't need to lunge: too far away and you can't reach. During your attack, it is only necessary that you stringer the debole of your partner's sword in a straight line, with the forte of yours. Be very careful to maintain opposition from the moment you are in wide measure, through to the moment you strike, and as you recover. It seems a little artificial to set up a strike at this distance: Capoferro explains that a strike at this measure normally occurs when either you are late, or your opponent attacks furiously, and the wide measure is crossed before you can act (Table 112).

Wide measure:
1. Partner stands on guard in terza.

2. Enter into wide measure, stringering your partner on the inside as above.

3. Fully extend and lunge. Hit the chest.

4. Recover, maintaining opposition.

Feel free to replace this exercise with any other drill you know that involves you lunging.

Notes

The Three Tempi in the Footwork Form

Moving forwards is easy. Retreating under cover without sacrificing your structure is much harder. And moving forwards again after moving backwards is even more difficult, and basically impossible if you have sacrificed your structure when moving backwards. Changing direction, especially backwards to forwards, is a critically important fencing skill. Because Capoferro has an example in the book of striking while stepping backwards (in his description of the narrowest measure), we start with that: step back while thrusting at the arm. Then, because this is training, step back and lean, then step back and lunge.

This combination will almost certainly *never* happen in an actual fight. We have it for the following reasons:

1. It's a reference to the text

2. which is easily modified to teach a critical skill (changing direction)

3. and it's very hard to give the proper coaching signal to your partner if doing a pair drill, so we can use this sequence as a coaching training tool (more on that in the next workbook).

So this bit of the form goes:

1. Step back and thrust at the arm

2. step back and strike with the lean

3. step back and strike with a lunge, and recover *forwards* with two passes.

The recovery forwards is there so that a forwards recovery is included somewhere in the form; it's a necessary skill for chasing down hesitant opponents, but Capoferro doesn't mention it.

So now you have the first three 'steps' of the form: Plate 7, Plate 8, Three Tempi. Put it all together, and commit it to memory…

Notes

Plate 17: Scanso del Pie Dritto

This plate shows the *scanso del pie dritto,* the void of the right foot. It is a fast and effective way of getting your entire body out of the way of an attack to your inside line. The set-up is the same as for Plate 16: you stringer on the outside, they disengage and attack on the inside, and you leap into action…

Plate 17 **Scanso del pie dritto** drill:

1. Stringer them on the outside

2. Partner disengages to thrust with a lunge on the inside, in quarta

3. Turn your hand to quarta, aiming at the bib of your partner's mask, under their jaw on the left side of their face ("near the ear" is specified in the source). Step slightly forwards and to the right with your right foot, turning it to point left. Lean back a little. Your point lands on their mask as your foot lands. You are far enough from their blade that it should pose no direct threat (there is no proper opposition).

This is my favourite play in this system: it makes me grin every time I do it. The attacker's technique is beautiful, and the counter to it even more so.

Of course, if your partner were a clever person, they would disengage with a feint…

1. As you are stringered on the outside,

2. Your partner disengages and feints in quarta

Page 31 of 80

Notes

3. You are 'fooled' into attacking with the *scanso dell pie dritto*

4. They drop their point over your sword, binding you to the outside, passing with the left foot, and strike you in the flank, grasping your sword hand. This is exactly like the *scannatura*.

Although the voids or avoidances (*scansi*) are illustrated only on plates 17 and 19, they have actually been used in some of the earlier plates, as counters to the actions shown on plates 9, 12, and 18.

Plate 17 Scanso del Pie Dritto
https://guywindsor.net/blog/rbc207

The Rapier Footwork Form, part one complete

Well done! You now have all the components of part one of the Footwork Form. Part one ends with the *scanso del pie dritto* because we needed to turn round and face the other way, to make the form fit into the salle across its narrowest point. This makes having a class of students doing the form at the same time much easier.

Run steps 1-3 from memory, then add step 4: step forwards, and as your back foot touches the floor, execute a flawless *scanso del pie dritto*.

Now for the purposes of the form, pivot on the ball of your front foot (right for right-handers), turning round so you are facing back the way you came.

Got that? Here's a video clip just in case…

Part 1 complete
https://guywindsor.net/blog/rbc208

Now go play...

At this stage, you and your partner can:

- advance
- retreat
- lunge
- stringer on either side
- attack by disengage.

And you can counter the disengage with:

- a counterdisengage
- a parry riposte in one tempo
- a parry riposte in two tempi
- a scannatura
- a scanso del pie dritto.

Or you could respond to being stringered with:

- a feint
- a cut to the face (or leg, but you probably shouldn't)
- a stringering of your own.

You are accustomed to playing already, using the Hunt the Debole drill. So try adding some further degrees of freedom. For example, you could agree that one or other of you will stringer, and the other will disengage … but it could be a real attack or a feint. The stringerer is free to deal with what they get. See what happens.

You will almost certainly end up creating an unholy mess, if you're actually practising a bit beyond your comfort zone. So long as it's a safe unholy mess, and you stop before it gets really frustrating, it's fine. If you will be going at all competitively, you will need at least a fencing jacket, plastron, mask, and gloves, and make sure your swords have good rubber tips on them. For more robust play, add elbow and knee protection, and a coach's plastron or similar. You may not have the necessary equipment to fence yet; that's ok, you can learn much from more restrained play.

Freeplay kit video
https://guywindsor.net/blog/rbc209

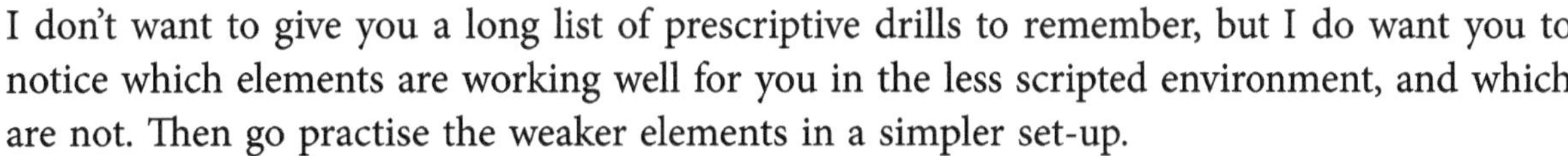

I don't want to give you a long list of prescriptive drills to remember, but I do want you to notice which elements are working well for you in the less scripted environment, and which are not. Then go practise the weaker elements in a simpler set-up.

In the next workbook I will be going into skill development in depth and detail, but as you may have noticed I believe in using play as early as possible, so go have some safe clean fun. If it provides useful insight, or motivation to practise, it's time well spent.

THE SEVENTH CLASS

DUCKING AND DIVING

To start with, warm up as usual, then pay particular attention to your legs and back: we will be covering the action on Plate 11, which is quite demanding.

Revise Plates 7 and 16, play a little Hunt the Debole, then go through the entire first part of the Footwork Form from memory solo, then plate by plate and play by play. Spend as much time, and as many sessions, as you need to to get everything in part one really solid.

Done that? Ok, let's have a look at Plate 11.

Plate 11: Contratempo

The organising theme of this workbook is the Footwork Form, which is itself organised by the kind of footwork each action requires. That is a perfectly sensible way to do it, but of course it is not perfect – not least because one footwork action can occur in many tactical contexts. Plate 11 is a perfect example of this. It contains five or six (depending how you count) separate plays which all end with the illustrated action, but you arrive there in the following ways:

* you offer a high blade to be stringered, your partner stringers, and you attack

* you are stringered on the outside, and disengage with a feint

* you are stringered on the inside, and disengage with a feint

* you stringer on the inside, and attack on their disengage

* you stringer on the inside, and parry their attack by disengage

* you stringer them on the outside, they disengage to stringer you.

Plate 11 drill one:
1. Partner stands on guard in terza

2. Stand on guard in terza

3. Move into "a high transverse quarta", pointing your sword at their left shoulder

4. Partner uses this as an opportunity to enter, stringering you on the inside

5. As they enter, turn your hand to seconda and strike, passing forwards with the left foot (this is not mentioned in the text, but is clear in the illustration), dropping down under their sword with the illustrated action.

Plate 11 drill two:
1. Stand on guard in terza

2. Partner comes to stringer on the outside

3. Disengage and feint in quarta to their face

4. Partner attempts to parry (how is not specified; I do it with a simple shift to quarta, as illustrated)

5. As they parry, turn your hand to seconda and strike, passing forwards with the left foot, dropping down under their sword with the illustrated action.

Plate 11 drill three:
1. Stand on guard in terza

2. Partner comes to stringer on the inside

3. Disengage and feint in terza to their face

4. Partner attempts to parry "raising their sword"(I interpret this as a false edge strike, a half-cut of falso manco)

5. As they parry turn your hand to seconda and strike, passing forwards with the left foot, dropping down under their sword with the illustrated action.

Plate 11 plays 1-3
https://guywindsor.net/blog/rbc210

Notes

Plate 11 drill four (a):
1. Partner stands on guard in terza

2. Stringer them on the inside, in quarta

3. They disengage and attack in seconda to your face

4. As they attack, turn your hand to terza and strike, dropping down under their sword with the illustrated action.

Plate 11 drill four (b):
1. Partner stands on guard in terza

2. Stringer them on the inside, in quarta

3. They disengage and attack in seconda to your face

4. As they attack, turn your hand to terza and execute a sharp false-edge cut to their sword.

5. and drop your point under their arm, turning your hand to seconda, and lowering your body with the illustrated action.

Note the similarity of the parry with the one on Plate 7, though the prior actions and the riposte itself are quite different.

Plate 11 drill five:
1. partner stands on guard in terza

2. stringer them on the outside, in terza

3. They disengage to stringer you on the inside

4. As they turn their sword, drop your point a little and strike in terza, passing forward with the left foot, entering with the illustrated action.

Plate 11 plays 4-5
https://guywindsor.net/blog/rbc211

Now that you have the action of Plate 11 down, add it to the form. You've just turned round after the *scanso del pie dritto*. Step in to stringer, and pass offline, low and deep, and recover forwards.

Solo Training: Hitting Things

The Footwork Form is all about using solo training. Most of my own training is done alone. It's much more effective, I find, because the imaginary opponent in my head is perfect, and never lets me get away with anything. Also, I can kill them over and over, without going to jail. Solo training is also useful for getting your striking mechanics down.

One of the core skills of using the rapier is getting the point to go where you want it to. So far, your long-suffering partner's fencing mask has taken the brunt of it, but it's time you learned to hit *hard, fast,* and *in time*, as well as gently and carefully.

The principal tools we use for this are the wall target, the pell, and the buckler game. For heavier cutting weapons we also use a tyre, but that's unnecessary for rapier training. Let's start with the wall target.

The Wall Target

(I have adapted this from my rapier training manual, *The Duellist's Companion.*)

The wall target is a padded striking surface for thrusting at. We know that these have been in use since at least the late sixteenth century, when a primarily thrust-oriented style of fencing became common. I use it with every weapon.

I made my own target out of a piece of plywood covered with camping mat foam and a layer of leather. Additional leather patches to reinforce the target points are a good idea. Wall targets should be large enough that you are never likely to miss the target altogether; holes in the wall are hard to explain. The main school target has three main striking points, approximately

Page 42 of 80   ~ 116 ~

at face, heart and groin height (for an opponent standing on guard), with two additional points placed like eyes. There is enough space around the target for all footwork actions, for both left- and right-handers.

For any thrust-oriented weapon this is perhaps the most important solo practice you can do: in addition to accuracy, it teaches you distance, power, and control. Make sure before you start that your blade is designed to take the repeated bending, and if you are using a triangular section blade, make sure that the point of the triangle is in the inside of the curve. Symmetrically cross-sectioned blades (such as the common lozenge shape) can bend in both directions. Regular practice on the wall makes up about 80 per cent of my own rapier, smallsword, and foil training. It is very important that the blade bends when the point touches the wall, but there is no "give" anywhere else. Ensure that the blade stays in line with your forearm, and your wrist locks to support the pressure.

The purpose of the lunge is to drive the sword through the target. With a practice blade and a wall target, the energy is absorbed by the blade; with a sharp blade and a penetrable target, that energy is used to puncture the target.

The sword/swordsman combination should be perfectly aligned so that no energy "leaks." The lunge is the perfect long attack with all your weight and energy focussed in one direction, on one point.

Exercises on the Wall Target
Setting up, striking with the extension:
1. Establish your guard position, and extend your sword.

2. Approach the target and place your point on the marked spot.

3. Withdraw your arm to the normal guard resting position.

4. Extend in quarta and place your point on the spot (or as close as possible). You should be close enough that your blade bends convincingly.

5. Repeat ad nauseam, in prima, terza, quarta and seconda.

Setting up and striking with the lunge:
1. Establish your guard position, and extend your sword

2. Approach the target and place your point on the marked spot

3. Withdraw your arm to the normal guard resting position. Step back into lunging distance , and strike with the lunge

4. Repeat ad nauseam, in prima, terza, quarta and seconda.

Further exercises:
• Using every kind of footwork action you know (such as passing, plates 11, 17, 13, and so on).

Notes

- Using multiple targets: once you are reasonably successful at the above exercise, it is a good idea to practice striking at different marks, at varying heights, and from all guards. Try numbering the points and have a friend call out numbers randomly; you must strike that number as fast as possible.

- Starting from well out of range and approaching using correct form, to strike with a predetermined action (such as a scanso del pie dritto).

- For extra difficulty, you could fix a tennis ball or squash ball to a piece of string, hang it up, and try to hit it. After the first successful hit it gets much more difficult, because it's moving.

Point control is the hallmark of a good swordswoman. Practice it whenever possible.
When walking with an umbrella, pick spots on the pavement (litter, chewing gum marks, etc.) and tap them with the point as you go past. No one will notice, and you can get some useful training done while walking to the pub.

Point Control: the Wall Target
https://guywindsor.net/blog/rbc212

7

Notes

The Pell

The pell is a post, often with a crossbeam, fixed upright for you to cut and thrust at. Try the following exercises:

- Pick one blow, and see how hard and fast you can strike at the pell without touching

- Repeat with multiple strikes (use your imagination!) Strike fast, but stroke the pell gently on a marked spot (about as hard as you would like to be hit in freeplay). See how hard and fast that really is

- Repeat with multiple strikes in different lines

- Choose a specific strike, and approach the pell from far away, moving smoothly and without stopping with blows from guard to guard: see if you can arrive in measure with your sword in the right place to launch the pre-arranged strike. This is harder than it sounds.

- The 99 strikes exercise: Make 100 cuts at the pell, without touching it. Every time you touch it, the counter resets to zero. So if you touch on strike 99, you go back to the beginning …

The Pell
https://guywindsor.net/blog/rbc213

7

Notes

The Buckler Game

For this exercise we use a simple wooden buckler as a thrusting target. Your partner holds it in one hand (and wears a mask just in case), and offers it up for you to thrust at. Their job is then to make you move about, offering the target at various heights and distances, and for decreasing lengths of time, making it difficult for you to get the thrust in. This should be calibrated so that you can hit it about three to four times out of five attempts. Less than that, they should slow down; more than that, they should make things harder. This is just like using focus mitts with a boxing coach.

The Buckler Game
https://guywindsor.net/blog/rbc214

From here on, try to incorporate at least some time on the wall target, pell, and/or the buckler game into every training session. We have a version of circuit training you might enjoy:

Circuit Training

There are usually not enough wall targets for everyone in class to use at the same time, nor are there enough pells and other things (except bucklers – we have lots of bucklers!). So we set up a circuit with our two wall targets, a hanging target, a mirror, and the pell, which keeps five people busy, and equip the people left over with one buckler per pair or, if using a cutting weapon, add in a tyre or two as well. The mirror is used for slow, careful, perfect form practice. Everybody spends two minutes in each station, with a one minute warning so they can switch hands if they like (I do recommend it). One sadist has the stopwatch (usually me, though I usually take part in the circuits as well). We do one round, which puts everyone through the entire circuit, and takes between ten and twenty minutes depending on how many people are in class. That is usually enough!

THE EIGHTH CLASS

MAKE IT YOUR OWN

There is a lot to practise, and I see no sense in adding too much too soon. Start this session with a warm-up as usual, go through Plates 7 and 16 as usual, then revise Plates 17, 13, and 11.

Then go over the Footwork Form so far: Plate 7, Plate 8, Three Tempi retreating, Plate 17, turn, Plate 11 recovering forwards.

Next up is your old friend the *scannatura*, Plate 13. Having recovered from Plate 11, add that on: step into measure with your imaginary stringering on the outside, and then pass in, bringing your left side forwards, then recover forwards. No video, no help at this stage … if you can't get it from a simple word prompt, you need to go back and do some revision before moving on.

As before, this may well be enough material for several training sessions. Move on only when you're ready.

The Form continues with Plate 18, which looks like this:

Notes

Plate 18: Striking with the Pass

The set-up is quite simple: you stringer on the outside, and as your opponent attacks by disengage, you thrust at them in quarta, passing in deeply with the back foot, keeping your sword-side forwards (as you see in the plate). This is basically a variation on Plate 16. It continues with the counter, as usual: if your opponent had been a clever person, they would have disengaged by way of a feint, and as you came to strike, would avoid using the same action we see on Plate 19.

This brings you to a dilemma: should you have a go at the whole Plate, or just do the first action (steps 1-3: the stringer, the attack by disengage, the entering with the pass) at this stage and come back to the counter when you know Plate 19? It's up to you.

I've linked to the Syllabus Wiki video here, rather than something from the online course, just to remind you about that resource. But before you watch the video, try to reconstruct the play just from the description above – then compare what you came up with to my version.

When you are comfortable with this pair drill, ending in the thrust shown in the plate, add the action to the Footwork Form: step, pass deeply keeping your sword side forwards, and recover backwards.

Plate 18 Complete
https://guywindsor.net/blog/rbc215

Notes

8

Plate 19: The *Scanso della Vita*

Beautiful, isn't it?

This action is very simple to set up: simply stringer on the outside, and as they come to strike on the inside, pass your back foot out of the way behind you, and stab them in the face. Left-handers facing right-handed opponents will need to stringer in *their* seconda, on their opponent's inside, of course.

But if D had been a clever person, what would they have done?

Why, they would have disengaged to stringer, gaining control of your sword, and passed in, striking you in the chest in quarta. Or, disengaged with a half-mandritto to beat your sword, and cut a riverso to your face … just like in Plate 16.

Plate 19 Complete
https://guywindsor.net/blog/rbc216

Notes: The Form

8

If you chose to cover this plate before completing Plate 18, now go back and do that. Note how often the counters on one plate are countered themselves on another.

You now have all the elements of the Footwork Form: add this final step to the Form, by recovering backwards after Plate 18, and then stepping in to stringer, and executing the most graceful *scanso della vita* ever done by a human being.

Well done, that's the Form complete.

Ready for a challenge? Do the whole thing again, but with your other hand. Every pair drill, every step of the Form. At the very least, do all your footwork on both sides. This will prevent you becoming excessively lopsided.

Now here's a thought: *you remember that which you are ready to learn.*

Being able to recall the actions is a necessary first step in learning to do them properly, and in context.

Here's another thought. If every step of the Form is a chapter heading, how would you fill those chapters? What is each step of the Form truly *about*, and where will it lead you?

HOMEWORK

I assume you can count just fine, and have noticed with some dismay my tendency to skip over parts of the illustrious Book. You are missing Plates 9, 12, 14, and (keeping to the sword alone), 20. We also glossed over Plates 6 and 15 rather. Don't worry about the rest of them at this stage. I assume you have a copy of *Gran Simulacro*, in translation if necessary. What I want you to do now, is work out the plays on all those plates, on your own. No help from me needed. Once you have figured them out, write out every action on the plate as as separate drill, as I've done previously in this book.

My own interpretation of each plate is up on my Syllabus Wiki, as you probably know, so you can cheat if you want to, but don't. See if you can work it out from just the text and the pictures. I promise you this: there's nothing there you haven't already done in some context or another.

I've provided the plate image, the text in Wilson and Swanger's translation (with their kind permission of course!), and some space to doodle in to get you started. Where the plates are especially wordy (such as Plate 6) I have broken up the text into paragraphs, and left space for notes in between. The footnotes you see are by the translators, not by me. I do discuss these issues in *The Duellist's Companion*, but it would be best if you try to work with just Capoferro's text, the image, and your experience of this course so far.

Should you wish to video your interpretation, and email me a link to it, I'd be delighted to see your work…

Notes

Plate 6

WAY OF GAINING THE SWORD ON THE INSIDE IN THE
STRAIGHT LINE AND STRIKING ACCORDING TO THE POINT THAT THE
ENEMY WILL GIVE

There are two reasons (it seems to me) for which it is necessary to draw close[1] to the adversary: the first is to stringer the sword in order to seek measure and tempo; the other is to draw close to the body of the adversary in order to seek only measure; which closings are best considered in the straight line; and because there are two causes of closing there must also be two occasions:

The first occasion, of stringering the sword in order to seek measure and tempo, is when the said adversary lies in an oblique line, because the adversary lying with the sword in quarta which is aimed on an oblique line at your left side, you lying with your sword on the outside, will disengage with an increase of pace in order to stringer it on the inside with the said straight line, as the figures show you; nor must this cause you any sort of difficulty, seeing as how only the said straight line suffices to stringer the sword when finding the adversary's sword lying in an oblique line. [Translation by Wilson and Swanger]

[Plate 6 continues…]

---

1 Note that the term "stringere" is used in this passage for both drawing close to the body of the enemy ("stringere la vita"), and in the sense of stringering of the sword ("stringere la spada"). This has made the translation somewhat awkward; I have translated "stringere" as "draw close" or "stringer", and rendered "stringimenti" as "closings" in this passage, to reflect these different meanings, although the verb is identical in the original.

Notes

[… Plate 6, continued]

The second occasion, that of drawing close to the body in order to seek only measure, is when the adversary lies in the straight line, or with his body uncovered; then without stringering the sword in order to seek the tempo, it will suffice to only draw close to the body with the straight line in order to find the measure, and then to strike according to the point; although the use of the art requires that one stringer the sword in all the lines without any utility.

Striking according to the point, one must understand, that every time that the point of the opposing sword is in your presence then you will be able to strike in the straight line where the height of the point of the enemy's sword will give its direction, taking a palmo from the point of your enemy's sword, however, with the forte of your sword, and you will strike safely, taking heed that if it is as high as the middle of your head you will strike him in the face, and were it even with the middle of your body you will be able to strike him in the face or the chest. This is called "to strike according to the point that the enemy's sword will give"; moreover in this way you will be able to safely disengage the sword from all sides in order to attack; however, when disengaging you will carry the forte of your sword in primo tempo to the point of the adversary's sword, and do not do as some masters do, who disengage, and do so in order to strike in primo tempo, arriving with the point of their sword on the forte of the enemy's sword, not perceiving that they give the point to the enemy, and most of the time they are offended, as is seen in our figures. [Translation by Wilson and Swanger]

Notes

Plate 9

A FIGURE THAT STRIKES IN A PASSATA WHILE THE ADVERSARY
DISENGAGES IN ORDER TO STRIKE

Figure D having gained the sword on the inside of the figure marked as C, the same C disengages to give a stoccata to the face of D. D strikes him in the face in seconda with a passata, giving a grip with the left hand to the hilt of the enemy's sword.

I will never fail to say that if C had been a shrewd person, he would have disengaged the sword as a feint with his body held back somewhat to the rear, and D approaching confidently to pass, C falsing underneath the enemy's sword and turning an inquartata with a void of the body, passing his leg crossed behind, would strike him in the chest. [Translation by Wilson and Swanger]

Notes

Plate 12

FIGURE THAT PARRIES WITH THE SWORD WITH BOTH HANDS AND
STRIKES WITH A THRUST TO THE THROAT WITH A PASSATA WHILE THE
ADVERSARY DISENGAGES THE SWORD

Figure D having gained the sword of the figure marked as C on the inside in low guard, and the said C disengaging to give a stoccata to the chest of figure D, D passes with the left leg and at the same time, pressing the enemy's sword down with both hands, strikes him in the chest in terza.

But without any doubt, if C had been an intelligent person, when he disengaged the point to attack he would have disengaged somewhat retired, and D, parrying and passing with both hands to strike C, C only with a lowering of the point of the sword toward the earth and turning his hand to seconda, somewhat voiding his body toward the left side of the adversary and disengaging the edge over the enemy's sword, will strike him on the inside with a riverso to the face, retiring into terza; or having parried, he will pass to the inside with the left leg; turning the body to the right, and holding his sword with both hands, while turning he will give him a thrust to the chest, going to him so that D cannot be saved. [Translation by Wilson and Swanger]

Notes

Plate 14

FIGURE THAT STRIKES UNDER THE SWORD OF THE ENEMY IN CONTRA TEMPO WITHOUT PARRYING, ONLY WITH A LOWERING OF THE BODY AS THE FIGURE DEMONSTRATES

Figure D having gained the sword of the figure C on the inside, and the same figure C disengaging to give a stoccata to the face of figure D, D lowering his body and stepping forward with his right leg in one same tempo strikes him in seconda below the enemy's sword in contra tempo without parrying as the picture shows.

And moreover he could succeed were the said thrust done differently, that is, that C disengaging to give a stoccata to figure D in the face, D parries in terza with the point high and in the same tempo lowering the point and turning the sword to seconda he could strike him in the chest with a passata while also giving him a grip on his sword hand.

But if C was an experienced person he could have only withdrawn his right foot to the rear and in his approach, meeting the enemy's sword on the outside and in the same tempo lowering the point and turning the hand to seconda he would strike him with a scannatura below the enemy's sword; alternately, in his withdrawing, he will parry with his left hand from above downwards under his arm and will strike D with a high seconda to the chest or to the face. [Translation by Wilson and Swanger]

Notes

Plate 15

DOUBLE MODE OF GAINING THE ENEMY'S SWORD ON THE INSIDE AND THE OUTSIDE

Knowing through experience how useful it is to know how to gain the enemy's sword, I have not wanted to fail to describe the manner which one must adopt in going to stringer and gain the same, and first, wanting to go to stringer the adversary's sword, on the inside as on the outside, according to the occasion, you will first have to stringer the same at a distance of about one palmo from the point; if it occurs that you have to stringer on the inside, you will make the point of the sword aim at the adversary's right shoulder; and if on the outside, at the left shoulder. Having done so, you will go walking towards the adversary's sword; if it occurs that he disengages, in that instant you will counter-disengage with a return of your sword to its place, or with the same counter-disengage you will strike him in the tempo of his disengage. [Translation by Wilson and Swanger]

[Plate 15 continues…]

Notes

[... Plate 15 continued]

Moreover, if it occurs that the adversary approaches in order to stringer your sword, on the inside as well as the outside, which is lying level in the straight line with your arm extended, in that instant you will disengage and stringer, walking forward; and if it occurs that you have to disengage in order to stringer on the inside, you will carry your right foot forward during the disengage, bending your body toward your right side, holding your left hand near your right, and then passing with your left foot, you will strike him with a thrust in the breast in quarta; and if you have to disengage in order to stringer on the outside, you will in a similar manner carry your right foot forward with a bending of your body to your left side, and passing with the left foot, strike the chest in seconda. Moreover, be aware that the following figures demonstrate stringering the sword on the outside in terza; however you must follow the rule of gaining the sword of the adversary as stated above. [Translation by Wilson and Swanger]

Notes

Plate 20

FIGURE THAT STRIKES THE FACE IN SECONDA ON A PASSATA GIVING A
GRIP TO THE SWORD ARM OF THE ENEMY WITH THE LEFT HAND

By clarification of the following figures, C, having his adversary, that is, the figure D, stringered to the outside, and the same D disengaging to give a stoccata to figure C, the same C parries the enemy's sword in quarta with a beat of the right foot, and all in one tempo, passing and turning the body well, he will strike him in seconda in the face, although this can also be done without passing, striking him in quarta although in due tempi.[2]

But if D had been a person experienced in swordplay, when C disengaged to parry figure D in quarta[3] with a beating of his right foot, D would have counter-disengaged his sword to the outside and would have struck him in the face in seconda, withdrawing to the rear into terza, following the enemy's sword with his sword in said withdrawing, and thus would C be struck. [Translation by Wilson and Swanger]

---

2 For clarification of the footwork accompanying primo tempo vis-à-vis dui tempi parries, see "Explanation of some terms of fencing" #7, "Of the parries".

3 This passage presents some difficulty. C is not described as disengaging in the beginning of this plate, only as having parried in fourth (which would not require a disengage since D was described as having begun on the outside and then disengaged to attack). It is possible that the subsequent "counter-disengage" by D is D's own return to outside stringimento following an initial disengage to the inside by way of a feint.

HIERARCHY OF DEFENCE

It's useful to have a clear understanding of the hierarchy of defence for whatever system you are training. This is a list of what counters what, in your system. I've started one here for you:

Action	Counter
Attack (cut or thrust)	Parry riposte in a single tempo Parry riposte in two tempi Avoid and strike
Parry riposte in a single tempo	Feint, parry riposte in two actions
Counterdisengage	Redisengage or attack
Stringering	Counterstringering Attack Disengage-attack Disengage beat attack
Counterstringering	As for stringering
Beat attack	Deceive beat (disengage in time), attack After beat, parry the attack in two tempi
Parry (in its own tempo)	Feint-disengage
Counterattack	Parry, riposte in two tempi

It would be a useful exercise to work through all the actions that you know in some detail, and create a complete hierarchy of defence. You immediately noticed I've left out the cut to the leg, for instance. Where would that belong, and what counters it?

I'd recommend having four columns: Action, Counter, Plate and Notes. I've given you a blank table overleaf. I suggest you photocopy it while it's blank so you can run off as many copies as you like.

Hierarchy of Defence

Hierarchy of Defence

Action	Counter	Plate	Notes

THE RAPIER

Part 3: Developing Your Skills

— Workbook —

Guy Windsor

Published by Spada Press

© Guy Windsor and Spada Press 2019

ISBN: 978-952-7157-48-0 R1.1 Right-Handers
ISBN: 978-952-7157-49-7 R1.2 Left-Handers

This book belongs to:

…………………………………………………………………………………

Date begun: …………………………..

Date completed: ……………………….

TABLE OF CONTENTS

DEVELOPING YOUR SKILLS

Welcome to the next level.

The goal of this workbook is to teach you how to train: how to take things you already know, and make them actually work under pressure. To become a swordsman/swordswoman/swordsperson, not just someone who knows some sword moves. This is the heart of swordsmanship, and its most sophisticated element. The key skill you will be learning is how to coach, because that's how your training partner will get better. And as they learn the content of this book themselves, they can coach you.

This is the difference between evolution by natural selection and intelligent design. If you just fence, sure enough you will get better. Slowly, and in a haphazard way. But using the skills you will learn in this book, you can deliberately work on your areas of weakness, find and enhance your natural areas of strength, and deliberately, intelligently, improve.

Birds are amazing examples of the awesome power of evolution. But compare them with the history of powered flight. By the application of intelligent design, we got from a short hop of 120 feet in 1903, *to the moon in 1969*. This is the kind of astonishingly rapid improvement that we are aiming for in this workbook.

We get there by building a bridge between your current level (which should be that you know Capoferro's rapier plays quite well, and have reasonable footwork and blade handling skills) to where you wish to be: expert fencer.

It is relatively easy to teach set drills to a student or class: she does this, you do that. And it is relatively easy to set up a freeplay (sparring, fencing) environment that is reasonably safe. I have seen many groups and schools that have nice set drills, and freeplay quite a bit, but there is no real relationship between the two kinds of training, and nothing in between those two extremes. As a result, the things done in freeplay bear scant resemblance to the actions in the drills. In this workbook I will show you how to build a bridge between set drills and freeplay. This is especially important for historical swordsmanship, as the manuals tend to show short, simple sequences (usually an attack and its defence) which are easy to turn into drills, but very hard to pull off in friendly freeplay or against a resisting opponent.

In a nutshell, you need to be able to identify your areas of weakness, and fix them. We do the former by running diagnostic drills, and the latter by training at the optimal rate of failure.

Most of this book will be about ways of running diagnostics, and of generating the optimal rate of failure in practice.

Run a Diagnostic

Almost any drill can be used as a diagnostic. The purpose of a diagnostic drill is to establish at what point you are failing. Taking Plate 7 as an example, by running through it you may find that you don't remember the drill (solution: learn the choreography. Refer to the first workbook), or one part of the drill isn't as good as it should be. Your disengage, for example. Or your parry. It doesn't matter which, it only matters that you can find it.

If the drill appears to be solid, with no obvious areas of weakness, then you need to train it at a higher level of complexity. I'll describe systematic processes for increasing complexity later in this book, so you will be able to ramp up the difficulty until something starts to break, i.e. you are getting hit, or you are staying safe but failing to hit.

To know where the drill is breaking, you will need clear feedback mechanisms.

Feedback mechanisms

The best feedback mechanism is a partner who will invariably hit you when you make a mistake, and who you will invariably hit without getting hit, when you do something right.

That partner is a coach.

But nobody is perfect, so your training will be slowed down by false positives, when you hit with things that shouldn't work, or your partner fails to hit you when you've left an opening, and false negatives, when you're doing the right thing, but your partner prevents it from working in a way that isn't useful for your development.

Secondary feedback mechanisms include video cameras, so you can see what actually happened, and verbal feedback from coaches and training partners.

Direct, immediate, and accurate feedback is the holy grail of training. Quest for it.

The optimal rate of failure

The optimal rate of failure is usually around two failures out of ten repetitions. This gives the optimum balance between encouraging success, and avoiding the boring self-indulgence of training at a uselessly low level. Improvement requires challenge, but too much challenge leads to frustration.

Mihaly Csikszentmihalyi's discussion of flow states is essentially describing the same issue, and his chart on page 74 (of the 2008 Harper Perennial Paperback edition of *Flow*) shows the training process (his example is of playing tennis, but it applies to just about everything).

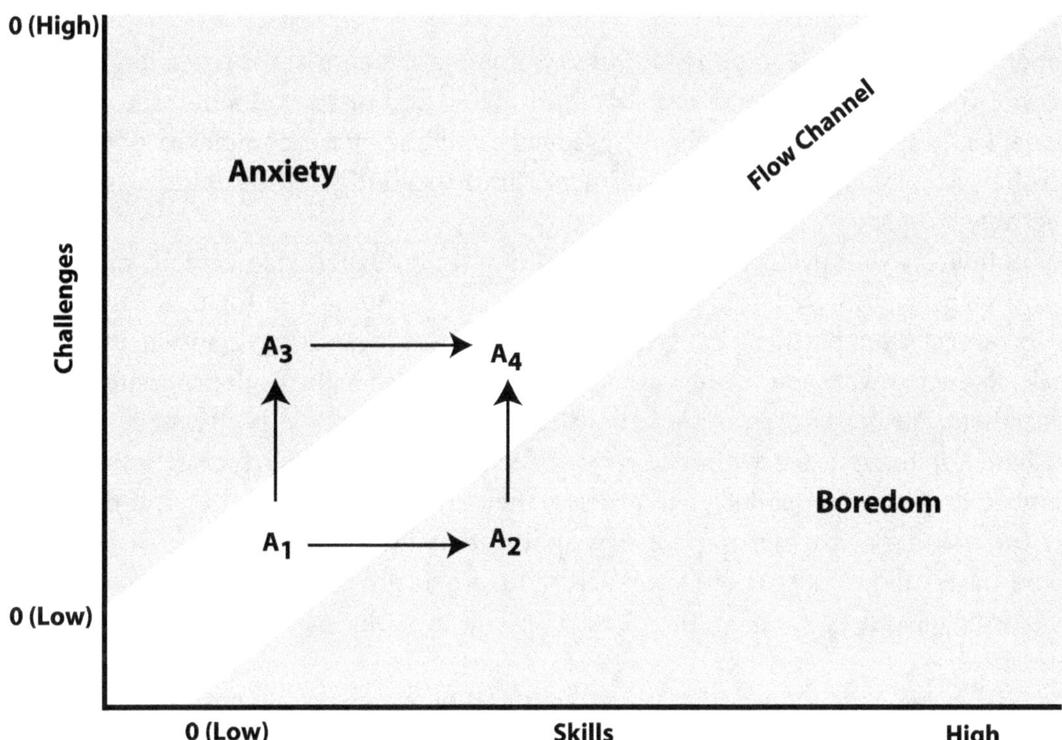

In the beginning, everything is challenging, so boredom and frustration are unlikely (assuming a competent instructor). After a while, the same basic drills are no challenge, so boredom sets in, and the challenge level must be increased; or the challenge level is increased too soon, so the student gets frustrated (or, in Csikszentmihalyi's terms, "anxious"). My goal in every teaching situation is to keep students in the optimal band between boredom and frustration, by adjusting the level of challenge accordingly.

Once your training starts to become seriously effective, it will inevitably start to expose weaknesses in your general psychological makeup – indeed, that's one of the key benefits of martial arts training. You should be aware of this before you jump in, and I've laid out some of the more common issues below.

Common Psychological Impediments

The main personal challenges I've seen facing martial artists getting themselves ready to train at a higher level are:

- Fear of injury

- Fear of embarrassment

- Fear of loss of control.

Fear of injury

Beginners should run little to no risk of injury; if you do, then there is something wrong with the school you're training at and you should probably find or start a better one. So this is an irrational fear, and should be handled by gradually building up the complexity of your training (I will show you how to do that in a moment) until you find yourself doing a "set drill" that is effectively freeplay.

Fear of injuring your partner is also very common (in my experience, actually more common than fear of getting injured yourself). There are several approaches for this. First, you must learn to respect your partner's integrity and sovereignty. It is up to them whether they take the risk of fencing with you. If they are keen, and your behaviour is appropriate, then if you do hurt them, it's not entirely your fault. Those risks ought to be pretty small, but nobody trains hard for many years without ever accidentally hurting a partner at least a little bit. Remember how you feel about your bruises; they are part and parcel of training, and you accept the risks. Your partners have every right to take the same risks.

If you have valid doubts about your ability to physically control your weapon under the stress of more advanced training, then I recommend the Pell, which you will find in part two of this series.

If you have still have valid doubts about your ability to remain in control of yourself when training, then don't do it. In my salle, nobody is ever *required* to do freeplay or more advanced drills. Had a frustrating day and think you might take it out on someone? Don't fence. Too tired to think straight? Don't fence. I have a scar on my scalp from the time I persuaded a friend to fence me, against his better judgement. He said he was too tired. He was right. I got three stitches. I have bled so you don't have to.

Fear of embarrassment

You will probably suck at fencing the first hundred times you do it. I did. So did everyone else I know. In any well-run group or school, you will get respect for putting yourself out there, training hard and trying hard, far more than you will for any actual skill or fencing success. People who laugh at beginners are arseholes. Ignore them, then surpass them. They do not deserve your attention, far less your embarrassment.

Fear of loss of control

This is tied up with fear of injuring your partners through accident or loss of self-control, and fear of getting injured yourself. At the end of the day though, set drills can become a crutch that replace training. If you are uncomfortable, and struggling at the edge of what you can do, then you are probably learning and growing. Comfort is for the pub after training, not the salle.

Sports psychology is a gigantic field, and I'm absolutely not a therapist. As a practical martial arts instructor, what I have seen to work best for the majority of students is simply this: create a training environment in which failure is embraced, in which effort is praised over attainment, and in which people feel comfortable handling the stresses of training in the way that suits them best. Hammering a heavy bag, sitting down for a quiet cup of tea, crying, or whatever else works and isn't dangerous to others. The best book on this subject hasn't been published at the time of writing, but look out for *Fear is the Mind-Killer* by Kaja Sadowski. I've read the first two drafts, and it's superb. Expect it out this year.

Equipment

You are going to need more safety equipment to complete the training in this workbook. At the very least, in addition to your sword and mask, you will need a puncture-resistant fencing jacket, a gorget, a fencing glove, and padding for the chest (either built into the jacket, or as a separate plastron). This is because you'll be training at the level where it is hard to control the level of impact. This video from the previous workbook may help:

Freeplay kit video
https://guywindsor.net/blog/rbc301

Building the Bridge

Every martial art I have ever come across uses set drills of some kind, even if only at the beginning (and in some cases, set drills *were the whole art*). Most of what you have done in the last two workbooks were set drills, such as reproducing Plate 7. Compare that with Hunt the Debole, a skill development game.

Whatever actions you are practising when you do a drill are usually specific to some kind of attack or action by your opponent. She thrusts to your face on the inside line, for instance. To start with I taught you to do this action slowly and co-operatively. And you have probably done it in freeplay (or seen more experienced people do something like it in freeplay). But it's likely that if you tried to do it in freeplay on day one, it would fail. That's not the technique's fault: it's because either:

* you did it in the wrong context, or

* you did it wrong.

We call the first problem "tactical", and the second "technical". Tactical problems are all about knowing the right thing to do, and technical problems are all about doing the right thing well enough for it to work. Most of the more complex training set-ups can go wrong at either point, so it's a good idea to have a clear idea of what kind of problem you are working on, and you should be able to identify the type of problem before you rush off to fix it.

Every drill should have a clearly defined tactical context, and a clearly defined technical solution.

Notes

The Pattern of Training

Run a diagnostic: train at the level where something goes wrong, then figure out what that something is. Is it technical, or tactical?

Then develop that skill, by training in ever-increasing levels of difficulty. You increase difficulty by increasing complexity, and/or speed and resistance. This is done using the following tools:

* Rule of C's

* Add a step

* Who moves first?

* Degrees of freedom.

This workbook will cover the next four classes, numbers 9-12. In the Ninth Class, we will address and practise the principles of good training.

THE NINTH CLASS

ADDING COMPLEXITY

In this class we are going to establish the principles of useful training. To begin with, warm yourselves up, and run through the Footwork Form, Hunt the Debole, and Plates 7 and 16.

9

Done? Ok, let's have a look at the fundamentals of skill development.

Start with the Buckler Game, making sure you both take a turn at being the coach. Notice how easy it is to distinguish between success and failure. For the student, success equals hitting the buckler. That's it. For the coach, success equals the student getting visibly better at hitting the buckler. It's that simple. Complexity is added by playing with timing and measure, and the student rises to the challenge.

The student will only get better if the coach challenges her. You can tell whether the student is being properly challenged by their rate of failure. If they are hitting the buckler every time, they are not being challenged. If they are missing all the time, they are too challenged. The optimal rate of failure is about 2 out of 10. Too many failures, slow down. Too few, make it harder.

Now run the buckler game again, and be absolutely focussed on the rate of failure.

So what is the buckler game good for? When would you prescribe it to a student or yourself?

I'd say for the following ailments: poor point control, poor timing, poor footwork, poor judgement of measure.

Obviously, it is completely useless for teaching solid parries.

This is true for every drill: it will be good at some things, and useless at others.

So now let's run the game again, modifying it for those three things.

1. Version One: point control. Mark the centre of the buckler, or use a smaller buckler, or make the buckler move a bit more. The skill you are working on is the ability to put your point exactly where you want it. Not timing, not measure. How can you make it more difficult? Make the target smaller, or reduce the available time.

Page 15 of 50

2. Version Two: timing. Be really careful about how long the buckler is exposed for, and the rhythm of the exposures. This is not about reactivity, exactly. It's more about teaching the student to move as the target is being presented, not when it's already there.

3. Version Three: footwork. The goal of footwork is to get you to the right place at the right time with the right structure. Very often, having taken a step or two, you will have your weight in the wrong place for lunging (or for doing whichever other striking action you're working on). So make the student move, and try to expose the buckler when they are off-balance (tip: they should *never* be off-balance if their footwork is any good!). If their weight is on the front foot, they can pass; if on the back foot, they can lunge…

4. Version Four: measure. You can expose the buckler when the student is out of measure and they should ignore it. Too close, and they've let you get too close. Play with challenging them to recognise the measures in which they can strike.

Versions two, three, and four are obviously related, but they are distinct.

Notes

Add a Step at the End

One simple means to make a drill more complex is to allow the "loser" to counter the last step if she can. For instance, you set up the drill, and as the attacker counters the defender may, if she sees it coming and can think up something useful to do, counter the attacker's action.

Taking Plate 7 as an example, you could counter the parry riposte in two tempi by doing a feint-disengage. Step 5 then would look like this:

5. 5Stringer on the inside. Opponent disengages with a feint. Feint a parry-riposte in one tempo, and as they parry, disengage and strike.

Or you could simply parry the riposte. Step 5 would then look like this:

5. Stringer on the inside. Opponent disengages with a feint. Do the parry-riposte in one tempo. Opponent parries and ripostes. Parry their riposte and strike.

There is in theory no end to this drill, as every action can be countered. Add one step at a time, and stop when it becomes difficult to remember how you got to where you are. This uses a set drill as a starting point to set up a kind of slow freeplay. You can see an example of this in this video:

Now apply this idea to as many other drills as you like. Spend some time freeing yourself from the idea that the set drills are fixed in stone.

Notes

Add a Step at the Beginning

Now back to Plate 7 and add a step at the beginning of the drill. This could be as simple as having your partner coming towards you, and as they reach the edge of measure, stringer them. Or you could start on the outside, and as you stringer them, they disengage to stringer you on the inside. You then attack (or feint) by disengage.

Play with this for a while, then apply the same idea to the other drills.

You can of course also add a step at both beginning and end. Have fun!

Add a Step at the Beginning
https://guywindsor.net/blog/rbc303

Notes

Developing Fencing Memory

I hope that things went usefully wrong in the previous exercises. To be able to fix the mistakes, you have to know what they were, and for that you need to be able to remember them. This is a fundamental prerequisite for skill development; at least one partner must know what just happened. If you can't repeat it, you can't train it, correct it, recognise it next time, or defeat it. We call this "fencing memory", and we have a simple drill for training it. You will need it for every stage of building the bridge.

This drill works best with three fencers, an attacker, a defender and an observer. Switch roles after each phrase, to develop your ability to remember phrases you have both done and seen. You can replace or enhance the observer with a video camera if needs be.

1.   Designate an attacker and a defender.

2.   Allow free choice of attack and defence, but no continuations (attacker can't counter).

3.   Attacker attacks as they like, defender tries to defend. Notice who gets hit.

4.   First one, then the other, then the observer, describes in clear fencing language, in detail, exactly what occurred.

For example: "Mary was in *terza*, I approached and stringered on the outside. Mary attacked with a disengage with a thrust to my face. I tried to parry and riposte in a single tempo, but my sword got caught in her quillons, and Mary's thrust landed in my face". Then Mary describes what she thought happened "well, I started in *seconda*, and attacked with a *mandritto fendente…*" (you'll be amazed how rarely you'll agree with each other to start with). Lastly, the observer states what they thought happened. If the observer doesn't have a reliable fencing memory (and even if they do!), use a video camera too.

When one attack and one defence can be reliably described and repeated, add the attacker's counter. When that is easily recalled, then the defender can counter that, and so on. Once you have built it up so that you can accurately reproduce a phrase of at least six actions (three from each side), your memory is ready for useful freeplay.

When you are reconstructing what happened, it's usually best to start with the blow that landed, and work backwards from there.

There would be no sense in providing a video of this, as the whole point of the drill is you don't know exactly what's going to happen, so should not be copying an example.

Notes

THE TENTH CLASS

WHO MOVES FIRST?

Warm up as usual, and make sure your base is stable by running through the Footwork Form and Plates 7 and 16. Some aspect of those drills will be less stable than others, so spend some time working on whatever stands out as needing work.

In other words, run a diagnostic, fix the weakest link.

This should get you into the proper frame of mind for what's coming up. I need you focussed on making measurable improvement to a specific skill.

Who Moves First?

Let's take Plate 7 as an example. In the basic form of the drill, if you are stringering, it goes like this:

1. you and your partner are standing still out of measure

2. you step forwards into measure to stringer

3. your partner attacks by disengage (or feints)

4. you parry-riposte in one tempo

5. your partner parries and ripostes in two tempi, if they feinted.

In any set drill, you can add complexity by changing who moves first. In the basic set-up, you moved first. But your partner could instead be coming towards you, (as we saw in the "Add a Step at the Beginning" variation) , or you could both be moving. Capoferro says as much in *Gran Simulacro,* Chapter 11, On the Way of Seeking Measure, paragraph 106: "There are three ways of seeking measure; because I seek it either while I move and the adversary fixes himself, or when I fix myself and the adversary moves, or when I move and the adversary moves." (Translation by Wilson and Swanger).

So you can set up Plate 7 in at least three ways:

1. in the basic form, where you move and your partner stays still,

2. or have your partner come towards you,

3. or you are both coming forwards.

In my salle we spend a lot of time doing basic drills but starting from way out of measure. The trick is to arrive at the right time, in the right place, to do the initial actions of a particular drill, without exposing yourself. This is very hard, at the beginning.

Play with this idea; begin co-operatively, so starting from way out of measure see if you can both come smoothly forwards, and make the drill look perfect. Once you can do that, see what happens if you have opposed intentions. For example, you could be looking to get the stringering on the inside, at the moment that you are in measure, while your partner is trying to get you stringered on the outside.

This will quickly devolve into a mess, but so long as it's a safe and useful mess, there's no harm done. Just start again…

Who Moves First?
https://guywindsor.net/blog/rbc304

Notes

Degrees of Freedom

At any stage in any drill, a set of decisions have been made. Systematically allowing a different choice to be made by one player, on the fly, introduces an element of unpredictability for the other player. For example, we might allow the attacker to choose her counter to the defence at random. This can be either to develop the attacker's decision-making skills (so the defender is helping her), or to develop the defender's ability to adapt (so the attacker is helping her). When there is a choice like that to be made, we say there is a degree of freedom – the attacker in this case has one degree of freedom – one point in the drill where she gets to make a choice. The other has to respond appropriately in real time. By adding degrees of freedom one at a time, we can get all the way from set drills to freeplay. Common places to add a degree of freedom are:

- The defender doesn't have to wait for the attack, but can pre-emptively attack.

- The attacker can vary the type of attack.

- The defender can vary the type of defence (the most common change is from parry-riposte (two motions, one to defend, one to strike) to counterattack (defence and strike in one motion).

- The attacker can vary their reaction to the defence (e.g. feint, or parry the riposte, or enter on the parry, etc.)

Adding a degree of freedom immediately changes a drill from choreographical to complex. At this stage, we must also cover the 'Rule of C's'.

The "Rule of Cs"

The "Rule of Cs" determines how every drill can be practised.

1. In the beginning, you learn set drills by Co-operating in Creating Correct Choreography.

2. Once the choreography is smooth, increase the difficulty by increasing intensity, or introducing a degree of freedom, with one player adjusting the difficulty for the other to learn at their most efficient rate – if it works all the time, ramp it up - if it fails more than twice in ten reps, ease off a bit.
    This is called: Coaching Correct actions.

3. 3. Finally, the players each try within reason to make the drill work for them. This can be dangerous if it gets out of hand, so be careful, and wear full protection just in case. In practice, the more experienced fencer should get most of the hits, without departing from the drill. This is fine, and gives a good indication of whether your training regime is working. So: Compete.

Let's stick with Plate 7 as our example and run through a specific series of degrees of freedom, and apply the Rule of C's so you can see the idea in practice.

* In the basic form of the drill, there are no degrees of freedom.

* Set up the drill, but the one stringered can, at the moment of the stringering, attack by disengage, or feint. That is one degree of freedom.

* Start out with the stringerer obliged to attack in both cases. This makes for a nice choreographical drill.

* Once that is stable, then the stringerer *will only attack if they believe they have the tempo.* This is a second degree of freedom. The stringered's job is then to *sell the feint.*

* Now we must ask the question who is coaching who? Because if the stringerer is coaching the stringered, then they must adjust their response so that the stringered *gets better at feinting.* If it's the other way round, then the stringered must adjust their feint so that the stringerer *gets better at identifying feints from real attacks.*

* You can also play the drill competitively. Without changing the drill, but allowing these two degrees of freedom, you can compete with your partner. If you are stringering, you are just trying to get the tempo for the parry-riposte in one tempo; if you don't get it, don't go. Your partner will be trying to trick you into it, with the occasional feint.

There is a significant risk of this getting out of hand; be mindful as you play the drill competitively that you must stick to the constraints of the drill that you have both agreed on. Otherwise you lose track of the rationale behind what you are doing, and mistakes creep in that are difficult to spot and to trace back to their source.

The Rule of C's
https://guywindsor.net/blog/rbc305

Technical or Tactical?

In the previous drill, if you were pushing the envelope even a little bit (as you should have been!), then there will have been times when you made a mistake, and got hit. The question is why did you get hit? It was either:

a) you did the right thing, but not well enough

b) or you did the wrong thing.

We call the first problem "technical", and the second "tactical". Tactical problems are all about knowing what is the right thing to do, and technical problems are all about doing the right thing well enough for it to work.

So now run the drill again, until one of you gets hit when they make a mistake. Using your newly-developed fencing memory, establish what went wrong, and why. Was it a technical or tactical error?

Now reconstruct the problem as either a technical drill (with no degrees of freedom), or a tactical drill (which will always have at least one degree of freedom). The partner who made the hit is the coach, and it's their job to make sure their partner never gets hit that way again…

In your notes, make sure to record who got hit, why, how, and what you did to train out of it.

Notes

10

Coaching

I kind of dropped you in it in the previous couple of drills: I got you coaching without teaching you exactly how. So let's have a look at that specific skill. In any drill you must have a clear definition of success. In a tournament bout, that's winning within the rules. In a basic set drill, it's making the choreography as correct as possible.

In a coaching environment, the student's success is defined as getting measurably better at the target skill.

The coach's success is defined as: the student is successful.

Be very clear on this before moving on. If the coach is doing their job properly, they will get hit over and over. Because in fencing, the student is successful if, and only if, they hit the coach, but do not get hit.

The coach's job is to create an environment in which the desired action will work, and everything else will fail. Failure is defined as the student not hitting, and getting hit.

The coach is providing a feedback mechanism. If the student is performing the desired action at the desired level, then they will be reinforced by immediate success; if they do anything else, or do the desired action at an insufficient level, the student fails to hit, and gets hit.

This is why a good coach can get preternaturally fast results, because they can create and control a perfect learning environment, in real time.

In a perfect world, every historical fencer would have access to a high-level coach and spend much of their time one-to-one with her. In the real world, that's never going to happen, so you and your partner must learn the basics of coaching so you can help each other develop.

As with every other skill, you will get better with specific practice. So in this next drill, let's be clear about who's training whom. We are studying coaching, so it is the *coach* whose performance we really care about. We measure that performance by the improvement of the student.

Coaching the Attack by Disengage

I have been preparing you for this over the last couple of workbooks. Begin with the Buckler Game. The one holding the buckler is the coach. You've done this many times before, so pay attention to the mindset: the total focus on your partner's improvement. This is the mindset you'll need for the following exercise.

You're going to improve your partner's attack by disengage. This action occurs in almost every Plate in *Gran Simulacro,* so it's quite important.

1. Start by setting up a static, basic version of Plate 7 and Plate 16, steps one and two. You step in to stringer, your partner attacks by disengage. Make sure the choreography is there, and that you both know what you're going to be working on.

2. Then reduce the window of opportunity for the attack by disengage, by stepping into measure, and immediately back out again. Not fast, but no pause. The student has to time their attack for when you will be there in measure.

3. Then follow their attack with a strike of your own, in any line. They must be recovering, and parrying if necessary, after their attack.

4. Then have the student keeping measure with you, waiting for your blade action (taking the line with a stringering) before they attack by disengage.

5. Finally, have the student keeping measure, and remaining defensive after their successful (or unsuccessful) attack.

The coaching exercises we'll be doing in this book will generally follow this same pattern:

1. set up the basic, static, drill

2. reduce the window of opportunity for the target action, by either reducing the time it's open, or providing mechanical resistance

3. add a step: make sure the student is getting out under cover after striking

4. add movement: have the student do the action while moving (so the drill doesn't start with them standing still). Refer to "Who moves first?"

5. add both the step and the movement, so they have to do the target action while moving, and remain defensive after striking.

Coaching the Attack by Disengage
https://guywindsor.net/blog/rbc306

This is a much longer video than usual, as I go through the entire sequence.

THE ELEVENTH CLASS

ADDING COMPETITION

Warm up as usual, and run through your basics, with one objective only: find an area of weakness that you can ask your partner for a quick coaching session on. Does your parry-riposte in two tempi need work? What about slipping the leg? Or your counter-disengage? Spend perhaps ten minutes each coaching and being coached, on something you have identified as needing work.

Now I have an exercise for you that will develop technical skill.

The Compound Counter Riposte Drill

This exercise is a technical study. Don't take it too seriously as an exercise in how to murder people, it is more an exercise in how to control your weapon, understand how longer fencing sequences can be put together, and it also leads to a very useful flowdrill, which you can then use for training actions in a less stable environment.

It begins with you stringered on the inside or the outside (you'll do both sides eventually):

1. you disengage and strike

2. as you disengage and strike, your partner does a parry and riposte in two tempi

3. you disengage with a feint, and your partner parries, disengage and strike

4. your partner's solution to that is to take two parries, and riposte

5. you feint, disengage, attack, then parry and riposte

6. as you feint, disengage, attack, and parry, she feints after her second parry, disengages around your parry, and strikes

7. you feint, disengage, take two parries, and riposte

8. your partner takes two parries, feints, disengages and strikes, then parries and ripostes

9. you feint, disengage, attack, parry, parry, feint, disengage and strike. This is the fabled 'compound counter riposte'.

You can build it up, step by step, until it becomes a sequence like this: parry, parry, extend, disengage, strike, parry, parry, extend, disengage, strike. Over and over again.

Once you get to the point where the person who does the first attack (you as it's written out above) is doing a parry and riposte by feint-disengage, you have what is called a compound counter-riposte. The term comes from classical fencing; it's not from Capoferro. A compound action is one that includes one or more feints, a riposte is an attack done after a successful parry, a counter-riposte is an attack done after a successful parry of a riposte. Don't take the terminology too seriously, it is just useful to know where it came from.

Once you have the drill working nicely from a stringering on one side, start it on the other.

The Compound Counter-Riposte Drill
https://guywindsor.net/blog/rbc307

Notes

The Compound Counter-Riposte Flowdrill

Set up the Flow
Once the Compound Counter-Riposte drill is working in both directions, on both sides, turn it into a flowdrill by continuing the pattern: feint, disengage, attack, parry, parry, feint, disengage, attack, parry, parry, etc.

Break the Flow
Once the flow is working nicely, you can break it with any agreed action. A beat attack, scannatura, parry-riposte in one tempo, scanso, whatever you want to work on.

Counter the Break
Once you can set up the flow, and break the flow, you can practise countering the break. So whatever action your partner breaks the flow with, you are waiting for it, and it fails against your effortless, beautiful counter. At this stage the flowdrill is now an unstable starting point from which to practice *any* drill.

And of course, you should decide between you whether you're doing this co-operatively, or with one coaching the other, or competitively...

The Compound Counter-Riposte Flowdrill
https://guywindsor.net/blog/rbc308

Notes

Coaching the Parry-Riposte in One Tempo

If you find that you and your partner can improve each other's attacks by disengage using the coaching method in the previous class, you're ready to try coaching something a bit more sophisticated. If not, then don't try this until your basic coaching skills are ready for it.

The pattern is the same:

* First set up the basic action in a static drill,

* then increase the difficulty by limiting time or adding resistance,

* then add defence, then add movement,

* and finally add movement and defence.

In coaching the attack by disengage, you made the action more difficult using your control of measure, by stepping back, which narrowed the window of opportunity for your partner/student to make the strike. Now you are going to use your control of blade relationship to make the action easier or harder.

Set up step three of Plates 7 and 16, to make sure your student knows the parry-riposte in one tempo, as a counter to your attack by disengage.

Keeping the drill basically static, adjust your disengage to more or less aggressively find their debole. Make sure your structure and blade relationship are solid, so if they fail to catch your debole as it passes their forte in the disengage, their action will fail.

When their action is getting better, add a strike immediately after their successful parry-riposte in one tempo, so they have to recover under cover.

When that's good, add movement, then movement and defence.

Coaching the parry-riposte in one tempo
https://guywindsor.net/blog/rbc309

Notes

Once you have worked on that, just for fun, try running the drill competitively. You are obliged to attack by disengage, and they are obliged to parry-riposte in one tempo, and whoever's blade relationship is better gets the hit. When that devolves into a mess, figure out what's going wrong and fix it.

Slow Fencing

This is a really useful drill that gets you away from choreography but limits the chaos. Simply start from out of measure, and approach each other with the intention of striking. But you have to both move at half speed. Get hit, you lose a point, speed up, you also lose a point. You can use any and every action you know, and just play with it. If you find that you're laughing, that's good.

This gets you away from the formality of set drills and coaching, and allows you to be creative, spontaneous, and to figure things out. You go slowly so that you have time to try things that you're not able to do at full speed yet, and to make it easier to figure out what happened after a point is scored (through the touch or through violating the speed rule).

Spend some time on this at some point in every class from now on.

Notes

THE TWELFTH CLASS

SETTING UP FREEPLAY

Begin as usual: warm up, run through the basics, do a little remedial work to get you into an "I'm deliberately improving my skills" frame of mind, do some slow fencing, and then we'll move on.

Freeplay

Think of a drill that allows either person to attack or defend, to respond with any action, and adds as many steps as necessary so that the play will continue until a technique is successfully concluded, and is conducted in the 'competition' mindset (not choreography or coaching).

We call it freeplay!

Before you begin fencing, it is important to agree on rules of engagement. This is partly to ensure safety, and partly to create an environment in which you can learn.

Here are my rules:

1. Agree on a mutually acceptable level of safety. Wear at least the minimum amount of safety gear commensurate with rule 1.

2. Confine allowable technique to those within the limits of your equipment.

3. Confine allowable technique to the technical ability of the least trained combatant.

4. Appoint either an experienced student or one of the combatants to preside over the bout.

5. Agree on allowable targets.

6. Agree on what constitutes a "hit". Agree on priority in the event of simultaneous hits. Usually it is better to allow a fatal blow before a minor wound, but simultaneous hits should be avoided whenever possible.

7. Agree on the duration of the bout either in terms of hits, such as first to achieve five, or in real time.

8. Acknowledge all hits against yourself. This can be done by raising the left arm, or by stopping the bout with a salute, or by calling "Halt!" and telling your opponent where and how you think he hit you.

9. Maintain self-command at all times. If you find yourself getting angry or frustrated, stop.

The rules can be adapted further to develop specific aspects of technique: for instance, you may not allow any close quarters work at all, or even restrict allowable hits to one small target. The idea is to come to a clear, common-sense agreement before facing off.

One of the hallmarks of a good swordsman/woman/person is courtesy. It does not matter what you think of your opponent (though it is usually safer to overestimate their skill) but it is essential to your development as a swordsman that you cultivate a respect for the weapon and its use. All bouts, however informal, should begin with the salute. After the bout you should always shake hands. I often acknowledge particularly good hits against me with a quick salute, rather than just raising my arm.

Now in discussion with your training partner(s), write your own rules.

Notes

Freeplay as a Diagnostic Drill

Now that you have your rules, set up these drills, in a friendly but competitive way:

1. You approach, your partner waits on guard. Stringer as you please. Your partner can respond as they like. Stop when one of you gets hit, or the play gets messy.

2. Change the roles; let your partner approach, and continue as before.

3. Begin out of measure, and you may both approach; continue as before.

Notice how and why you're getting hit, or your partner is. After these three rounds you should have a very clear idea of at least one area in which you are weak, and one in which your partner is. Spend the next ten minutes or more working on your and your partner's weakest link, then run the three rounds of freeplay again. The possible outcomes are:

1. You have the same weakest link, and it hasn't improved. So try a different approach for correcting it.

2. You have the same weakest link, but it is getting better. So continue with the same training solution.

3. You have a different weakest link. Fix that. Then run the diagnostic again.

Many clubs run freeplay at the end of class – letting off steam after the formalities are over. I think that's sub-optimal. It's better to incorporate freeplay as just another part of the training programme, to be approached in the same ways as every other drill. For diagnostic purposes, it's best to freeplay *first,* then use the insights from the bouts to decide the topics of the class.

Freeplay Rules

12

Pressure Drills

You may have noticed that the core of my approach is to isolate variables. Technical complexity, for instance. Degrees of freedom, for another. Pressure drills are exercises whose specific function is to get you used to performing under, you guessed it, pressure.

- The most basic set-up has you with two partners, all three of you in full freeplay gear. Each will give you the same attack, alternating, 10 times each. You will defend against each attack as best you can. In theory, you do the same technique perfectly 20 times. Your partners' job is to keep you moving, keep you under pressure. They do not wait for you to sort yourself out after each action; as soon as your defence is done, the next attack comes in. That's why you have two partners. As fatigue sets in, you will tend to make mistakes and get sloppy. Ideally, you will find it really, really hard to defend yourself. Please note this is not defence against multiple opponents; it's a stress simulator.

- The next level has the attackers varying their attacks; one from the left with a cut and the other with a thrust, say; and you have to do two different defences correctly.

- Then the attackers can attack as they please, their only job to keep you working under pressure.

Of course, in whichever set-up, immediately after you were in the middle, you take one of the attacking roles, then the other, so on the fourth round, you're back in the middle again. Good luck. You know you've really done this when you've felt like puking into your mask.

It's an age-old secret of martial training that acute fatigue is a good mimic of combat stress. When your heart rate is up past 180 and your legs and arms feel like they are falling off, and you can still get your actions right, then you have truly learned something.

Because of the level of fatigue, generally we run these drills at the end of class, and note down what needs work – yes, pressure drills are also diagnostic drills.

Notes

Choosing What to Train: Breadth and Depth

At any moment you should be adding either breadth or depth to your art. Adding breadth means adding new material - new techniques, new concepts, such as moving on to rapier and dagger (which is in the next workbook). Adding depth means taking what you already know and making it actually work. Coaching is the most efficient way to add depth.

Most diagnostic drills are specific to either breadth or depth. The drill 'do I know the whole of the Footwork Form?' tests for breadth. The drill 'does my attack by disengage work?' tests for depth.

As you may have noticed over the course of these workbooks, I tend to switch back and forth. Start with a little breadth (teaching the beginners a couple of things), then let them work on those things until they are a bit more solid, then adding the next new shiny thing. Generally speaking, adding breadth is more fun for beginners because they can clearly see that they are learning something. But at the advanced levels of the art, it is *all* depth training. Once you know *all* the techniques (and once you break it down there really aren't very many), the rest of your training life is about getting those techniques to work. The cycle looks like this:

You can download a snazzy full-colour printable version of this flowchart to print out and hang on your wall here:

How to Train: a Flowchart

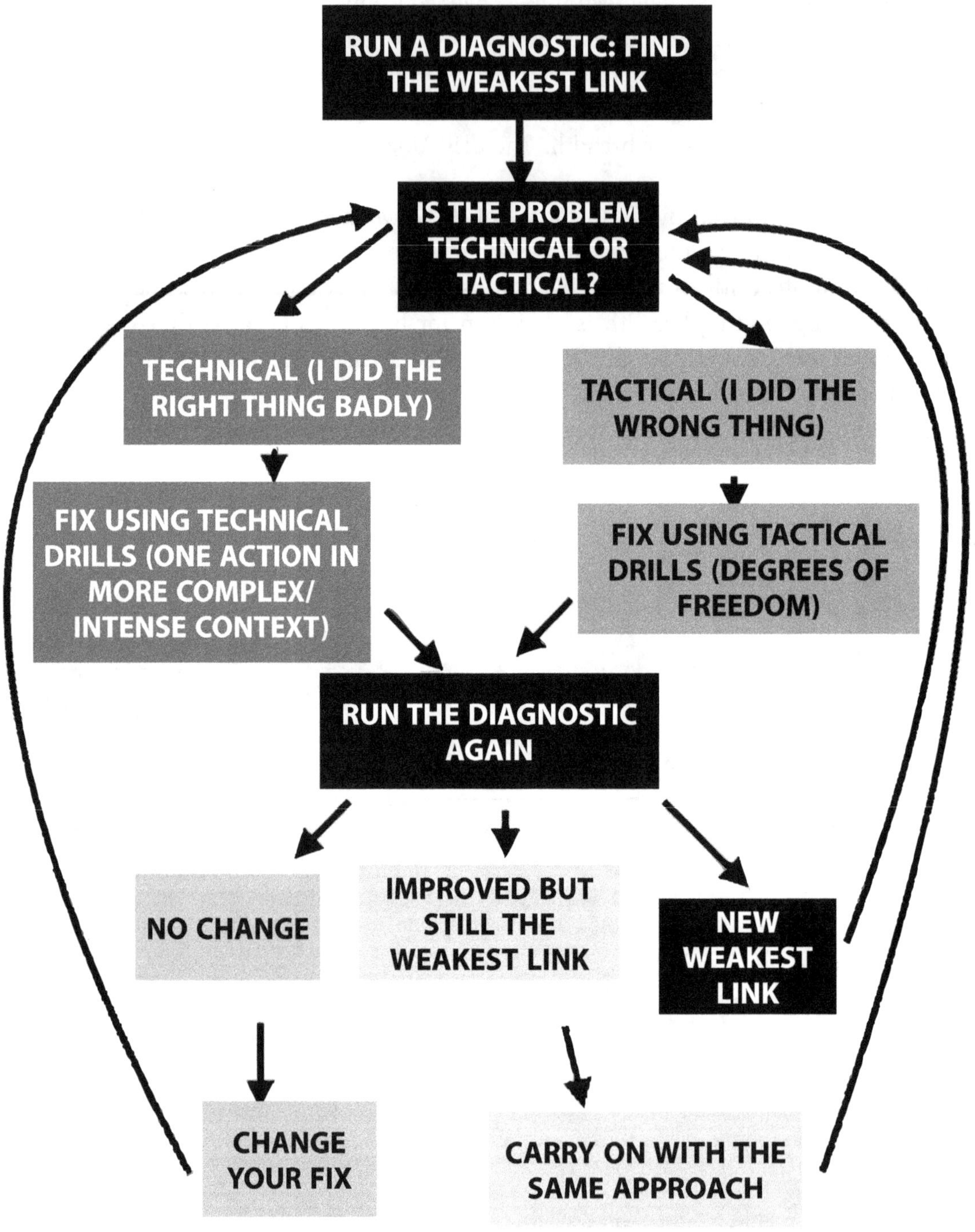

Let's take a concrete example, just to make sure this is clear.

Run a Diagnostic, find the weakest link

You run through the Footwork Form first solo and then as a series of pair drills and decide that step 2, Slip the Leg, is the weakest link.

Technical or Tactical?

Is the problem technical or tactical? Let's say it's tactical. You can do the slip easily when you know the cut to the leg is coming, but you can't do it otherwise.

Fix the weakest link

Set up a drill in which your partner will sometimes attack with a cut to the leg, and sometimes a thrust to the chest (or some other action). Have your partner coach you in recognising when the cut is coming. Success = slipping the leg. Don't worry about how well you do the slip, or how well you defend against the other action; the thing to focus on is only *whether you are slipping the leg when you should.*

Run the diagnostic again

Once it seems to be going much better, run the diagnostic (the Footwork Form in this example) again. Is step 2 still the weakest link? If no, then find the new weakest link, and start fixing it. If yes, is it better than it was? If there is no improvement, then change the coaching exercise. If there is clear improvement, just not enough, use the same exercises to improve it further.

You may have found in your Footwork Form that you just don't know one of the steps. That's a really good result, and easy to fix: just go to the particular chapter of Workbook 2 and fill in the gap. This would be considered a technical problem.

At every moment in your training from now on, you should be either running a diagnostic, or fixing the weakest link (your own or your partner's). There is no third option.

If you are spending sword-time just messing about and having non-productive fun, that's *totally ok.* But it isn't training, and don't expect to get better that way.

It's worth remembering that if you never have fun, you'll probably quit. But if you never improve, you'll probably quit too. So moderate your activities accordingly!

Notes

CONCLUSION

In this workbook I have laid out the fundamentals of my approach to learning swordsmanship. I treat every weapon, every system, and indeed every skill the same way.

We build the bridge between choreography and true skill with the following steps:

- Add a Step at the Beginning

- Add a Step at the End

- Who Moves First?

- Degrees of Freedom

- The Rule of C's.

- Freeplay

- Pressure Drills

When training, you are always either running a diagnostic, or fixing the weakest link.

By far the hardest part of this is maintaining the self-discipline to focus on the things that are hard, rather than messing about with the things that are easy. A large part of my job as a teacher is to gently redirect my students' attention back to where they know it belongs.

With this workbook you should become adept at adding depth. The next book in the series will add breadth: now that you are competent with the sword alone, let's add the dagger!

Rapier part Four: Sword and Dagger
https://guywindsor.net/blog/rbc400

If 'proper' books are your thing, then you should probably get the Duellist's Companion.

The Duellist's Companion
https://guywindsor.net/blog/rbctdc

If you prefer video instruction, then The Essential Rapier Course (from which many of the videos in this workbook came) might suit you better.

You can use this link to get 50% off the regular price for the Essential Rapier Course:

Rapier Course Discount
https://guywindsor.net/blog/RBC2018

There are of course many other instructors out there whose approach you may enjoy and benefit from, so don't feel obliged to limit yourself to just mine.

THE RAPIER

Part 4: Sword and Dagger, and Sword and Cape

— Workbook —

Guy Windsor

Published by Spada Press

© Guy Windsor and Spada Press 2019

ISBN: 978-952-7157-50-3 R4.1 Right-Handers

ISBN: 978-952-7157-51-0 R4.2 Left-Handers

This book belongs to:

………………………………………………………………………………………

Date begun: …………………………..

Date completed: ………………………….

TABLE OF CONTENTS

ADDING AN EXTRA WEAPON

Wonderfully romantic, isn't it? The flashing blades, the ting! ting! ting! of thrusts expertly set aside by a swift dagger parry....

Then the twitching corpse, blood pooling around it, and other matter, worse-smelling, as the body lets go in its final paroxysms.

Not so romantic now, is it?

I mention this because of all the weapons combinations commonly practiced in historical swordsmanship circles, the rapier and dagger is often most divorced from its reality.

Yes, we can train for display – stage combat is an excellent application of historical fencing skill. And we can train to be good at fencing our friends, or tournament opponents. Also time well spent.

But the root of this art is a bloody murderous past, where honour killings were common, and young men slaughtered each other in despite of the law, and to the despair of their kings. It's simply amazing to me that so much beauty would grow out of so much horror.

Okay, moving on.

As this is part four of a series, I hope it's obvious that you are supposed to be quite good at rapier by now. I strongly advise learning the rapier alone first, before adding the dagger. You'll see why when you try it: it adds a great deal of complexity.

Let's take a look at the dagger itself. Generally speaking, any longish knife would do the job, but historically, daggers intended for use with the sword were designed and made as part of a set, with matching furniture (no, not tables and chairs. Hilt furniture is the term given to the adornments of the hilt).

There is practically no end to people's ingenuity when it comes to weapons. This spring-loaded dagger from Philadelphia Museum of Art is an excellent example:

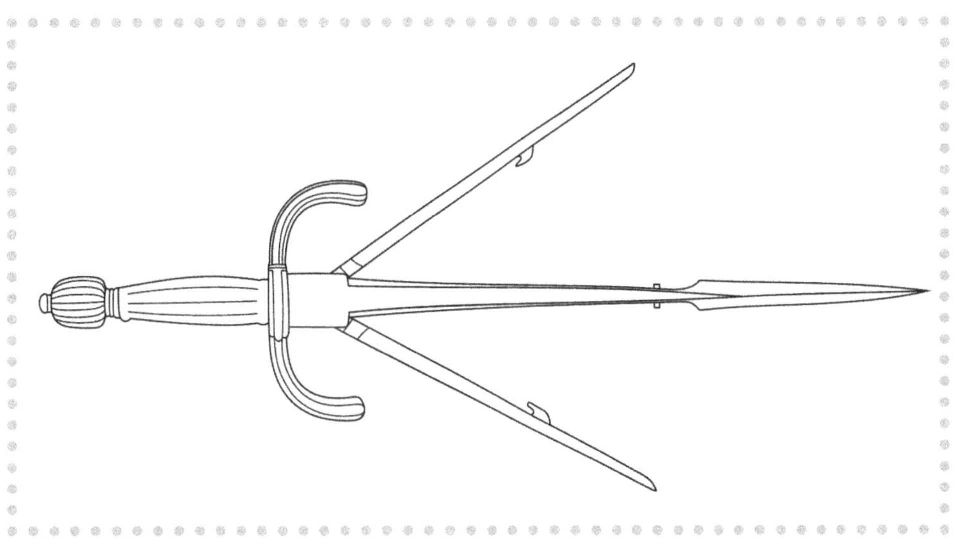

Due to copyright restrictions this is a sketch I had made, but you can find it on their website here: https://guywindsor.net/blog/phildagger1, and it is in their catalogue at Accession Number:1977-167-687. The point of the spring-loaded legs is to entangle the opponent's blade, giving you momentary control. My favourite take on this idea (because it looks so piratical) is this one from the Wallace Collection (catalogue number A867, on their website here: https://guywindsor.net/blog/wallacedagger1):

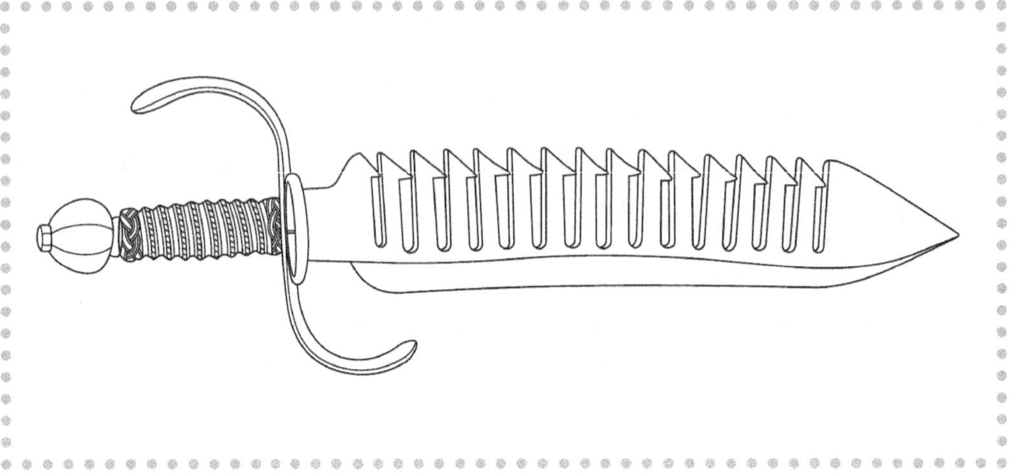

Each slot has a spring-loaded ratchet that will let a blade slip between the teeth, but not out again. In that moment you have control over the opponent's blade. Note, this is not a Rambo knife, and it doesn't work as a saw.

Most parrying daggers are quite simple, and have either a ring guard, like this one (Wallace A776):

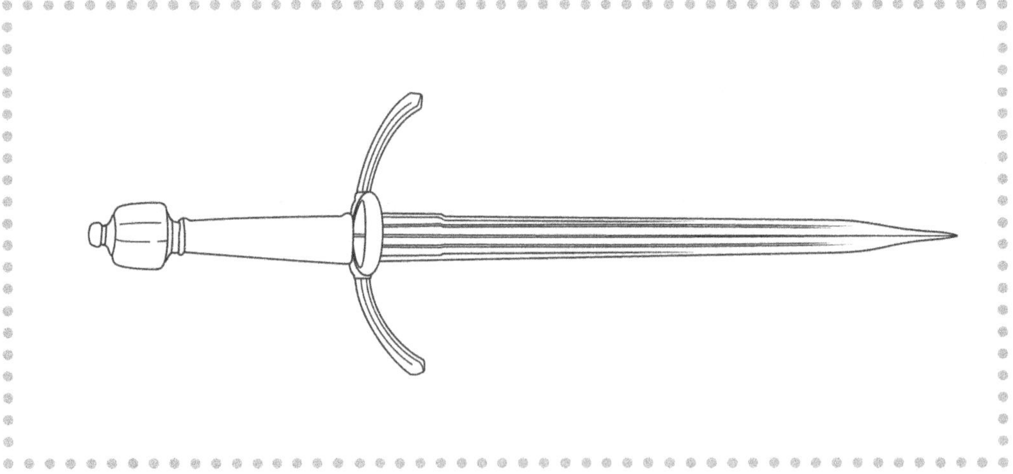

Or a 'sail' guard like this one (though they are usually Spanish, not Italian) (A826).

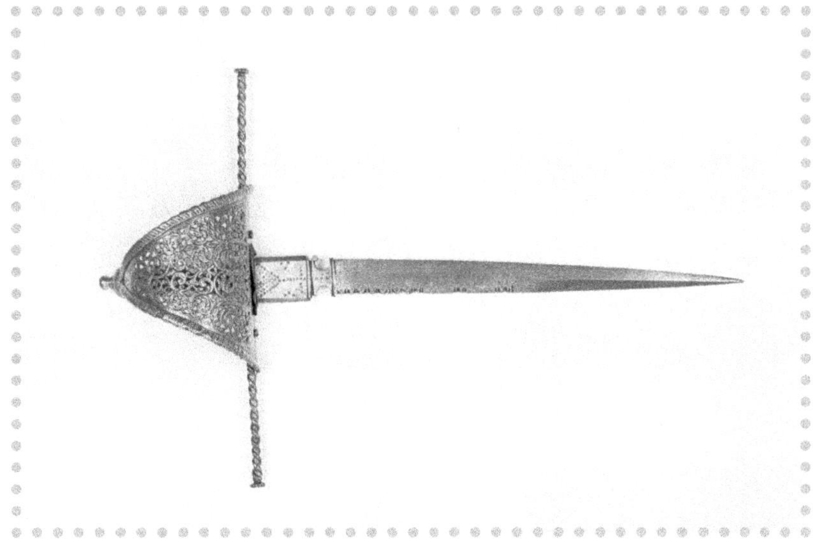

Our illustrious master, Capoferro, doesn't discuss the form of the dagger at all, and illustrates only very simple daggers, with no guards other than a simple cross, as you can see in this detail from Plate 27:

This also shows you the most common way of holding the dagger, with your thumb on the flat (as shown on the left), and holding it with your forefinger over the cross (on the right), something that is very hard to do with all historical examples I've handled (and reproductions), if they have a side ring, and impossible if they have a sail guard.

For our purposes then, you will need a parrying dagger with a blade of between 10 and 14 inches (25-35 cm), with whatever hilt you prefer, so long as it doesn't interfere with your grip. Sail daggers offer the best protection, but can lead you into lazy habits; simple cross-hilted daggers can lead to broken fingers if you fence too hard and miss your parry. I suggest learning and drilling with a simple dagger to learn good habits, and free fencing with a sail, to minimise the risk of injury.

As in the previous workbooks, I have divided this one up into four classes. Take your time, and go at your own pace.

THE THIRTEENTH CLASS

GETTING USED TO THE DAGGER

In this class we will cover the following:

- Grip
- Guard Positions
- The Dagger Parrying Game
- Plate 22

Warm up as usual, and run through some basic rapier drills, including Hunt the Debole, and Plates 7 and 16. Do more if you wish.

Holding the dagger

The dagger is held in the off-hand (right for left-handers), with either the thumb on the flat (most common), or the forefinger over the crossguard – the only justification for which is that it appears that way in some of Capoferro's plates. I don't recommend it. This raises the question of how reliable are those plates? On this evidence alone, we'd probably say 'somewhat, but not very'.

Holding the dagger
https://guywindsor.net/blog/rbc401

Guard Positions

There are six guard positions with the sword and dagger, labelled A through F, and numbered in the text (in Italian, obviously), first, second, third etc.

Plate 2 shows D, quarta, opposing A, prima.

Plate 3 shows B, seconda, opposing F, sesta.

Notes

Plate 4 shows C, terza, opposing E, quinta.

Go through the six guards, but don't spend too much time on them at this stage; you'll see them all again later.

The Guards
https://guywindsor.net/blog/rbc402

Notes

The Dagger Parrying Game

Setting aside a thrust with your dagger is a simple skill. Doing so while simultaneously thrusting accurately with your sword is more sophisticated. Doing so while simultaneously feinting and avoiding your opponent's parry with their dagger is even more sophisticated. So we will break this down into its component parts, and play with it.

This game has four levels:

* You use your dagger to parry simple sword thrusts
* You parry simple thrusts while striking with your sword
* You use your sword to deceive your partner's dagger parries
* You parry with your dagger while deceiving with your sword.

This is a *game*. You are supposed to have fun with it. And you must forget all about proper guard positions, proper lunges, and so on. If you happen to have them, that's fine, but no particle of your attention should be on anything other than the specific skill you are working on.

For all levels of the game, you should be using masks, and ideally jackets and other protective equipment. You should know how to dress by now!

Level one:
You have just a dagger in your off-hand, your partner has just a sword. Your partner just tries to stab you, and you parry. The thrusts should come in from every angle. Not too fast at first. When it's your turn to attack, you should aim to keep your partner training at their optimal rate of failure.

The dagger parrying game part one
https://guywindsor.net/blog/rbc403

Level two:
You have a sword and a dagger, your partner has just a sword. As they strike you (like in level one), you parry with the dagger, and strike with the sword (not too hard). The one attacking is coaching the defender to parry and strike at the same time.

Notes

The dagger parrying game part two
https://guywindsor.net/blog/rbc404

Level three:

You have just a sword, your partner has just a dagger. Thrust at them, and as they parry with their dagger, avoid the parry and strike. If they touch your sword before you hit them, that's your failure.

The dagger parrying game part three
https://guywindsor.net/blog/rbc405

Level four:

You both have sword and dagger. As your partner thrusts, you parry and feint at the same time. They try to parry your 'attack' with their dagger, you avoid their dagger and strike.

Work through the four levels of the game. This will be part of all of your rapier and dagger training sessions from now on. It's the rapier and dagger equivalent of Hunt the Debole.

The dagger parrying game part four
https://guywindsor.net/blog/rbc406

Notes

Plate 22

Let's have a look at the text, shall we? I'll be using the excellent Wilson and Swanger's translation throughout this book, as in the previous volumes. If you see Bill or Jherek in person or online, be sure to thank them.

FIGURES THAT DEMONSTRATE HOW WITH A SINGLE PARRY WITH THE DAGGER IT IS POSSIBLE TO STRIKE IN THREE PLACES With A Thrust, Namely In The Face, In The Chest, Or In The Thigh

These following figures demonstrate an artful manner of striking in three different ways with a thrust with a single parry of the dagger, which are done thus: that, in quarta, having the adversary stringered on the inside in whatsoever guard apt for stringering on the inside, he will be able to disengage to give you a thrust in two ways: to the face or chest; however, he having disengaged to strike you, you will parry his sword to the inside with your dagger over your right arm, and in the first occasion you will be able to strike him high or low, that is, to the face, or under the arm in the chest or in the thigh; and in the second only to the face or thigh.

As the image suggests that the adversary is in terza (note the 'C' by his left foot), we'll set this up like so:

1.   You are in quarta, your partner is in terza.

2.   You approach to stringer, just like in Plate 7.

3. Your partner disengages to strike, in your face or chest.

4. You parry over your arm with your dagger, and thrust. If they went for your face, you can strike them in the face, chest, or lead thigh. If they went for your chest, you can strike them in the face or thigh, because their sword is in the way of the line to their chest.

Plate 22

https://guywindsor.net/blog/rbc407

THE FOURTEENTH CLASS

BROADEN YOUR BASE

In this class we will cover plates 23-25, and plates 38 and 39, in some detail. Begin with a warm-up, run through the Footwork Form, do a bit of Hunt the Debole, segue into the Dagger Parrying Game, and finally revise Plate 22.

Ready? Great. We're going to cover a lot of technical ground. If it all starts to run together in your head, take breaks with a bit of slow fencing, with or without the dagger.

I will be including the text for each of these plates, because I want you to see the relationship between Capoferro's words and your actions. This will become especially important in the next class.

Plate 23

A FIGURE THAT STRIKES IN SECONDA IN THE CHEST BETWEEN THE WEAPONS BY A PRETENSE, DISENGAGING OVER THE Dagger, And Also In The Same Manner Could Have Struck In Quarta.

The adversary lying in a low terza with the arm withdrawn, and with the dagger forward and united with the sword, you will place yourself opposite him in a high terza, making a feint outside of the dagger to the face in a high quarta or a similar terza, and while he raises his dagger to parry and attack you in quarta, you will disengage over his dagger and, in the same tempo, parrying to the inside you will strike him in seconda in the chest.

Notice that your guard, your partner's guard, and most particularly the starting position of your partner's dagger, are all clearly stated. This is because they are extremely important in determining what will happen next. Notice also that when your partner parries, they also immediately and in the same motion strike at you. While they do that, you have to a) parry with your dagger and b) avoid their parry. This should be a very familiar idea, after playing the Dagger Parrying Game a few times.

You can set this up like so:

1. You are in quarta, your partner is in quinta, their sword and dagger low, hands next to each other

2. You approach in a high terza, and feint over their dagger

3. As they parry with their dagger and strike with their sword

4. You parry over your arm and deceive their dagger, striking them in the chest.

Plate 23
https://guywindsor.net/blog/rbc408

Notes

Plate 24

A FIGURE THAT STRIKES ABOVE THE RIGHT ARM IN THE CHEST AND MAKES THE SWORD FALL WITH THE UNFASTENING Of The Sword And The Dagger

From this figure you will easily be able to comprehend and learn the manner of casting down the sword from the hand and giving as well in the same tempo a thrust to the chest; that is, finding yourself in terza with your arm withdrawn and uniting your dagger with your sword, the adversary being in the same guard, or in quarta, you will commence to stringer his sword on the inside in quarta, and you will lower your dagger to the middle of your right arm in an oblique line; and your adversary disengaging to strike you in the chest in quarta, you will strike him from the outside with a punta riversa to the body, raising the hilt of your sword somewhat, and in the same tempo parrying downward with the flat of your dagger to the outside you will force him to abandon his weapon.

This is very effective, and you could break your partner's finger if you're not careful. I recommend that the one being stringered should take their forefinger off the crossguard for this drill.

You begin in "terza with your arm withdrawn and uniting your dagger with your sword". To my mind, that's exactly the same as quinta, so I'd say start in quinta. You will be stringering on the inside, in quarta. The critical part of the set-up is getting your dagger to lie over your right elbow, pointing to your right (for right-handers). This way, when your partner attacks, the dagger can push their sword over to your left (right for left-handers).

The specific mechanics of the disarm involves effectively wrapping your opponent's sword arm round your sword blade, using the leverage of your dagger on their sword to do it. It therefore works quite differently cross-handed. I recommend walking through this play same-handed; if your partner is differently-handed, you should both try it on both sides (left v left, and right v right). You should also have a go at making it work right v left.

Yes, it's long past time that you learned to use the sword in either hand!
Set it up like so:

1. You are in quinta, partner is in any guard you can stringer on the inside.

2. You come to stringer, letting your dagger come over your sword arm, as described above

3. As your partner attacks, thrust in quarta over their sword arm into their chest – don't parry with your sword at all

4. And at the same time parry their thrust with your dagger, over to your inside.

Plate 24
https://guywindsor.net/blog/rbc409

Notes

Plate 25

A FIGURE THAT PARRIES WITH THE DAGGER HIGH TO THE INSIDE AND STRIKES WITH A RIVERSO TO THE THIGH, AND IN Quarta To The Chest As The Figure Demonstrates

Finding yourself in quarta with the dagger high and your adversary in whatsoever guard apt for stringering on the inside, with the right leg forward, you will commence to stringer him on the inside in quarta, and he disengaging to strike you in the face in quarta, you, parrying to the inside with your dagger, over your right arm, will be able to strike him either with a riverso to the thigh or with a quarta below the arm.

This is another one of those magic swords that have spring-loaded blades that split so you can strike in two places at the same time…

Or maybe not.

I have included this play because it is a simple example of 'parry and strike in one tempo', and I want to make sure I included canonical examples of all the different dagger parries that we find in the source.

You can set up this play like so:

1. You are in quarta, with the dagger high, your partner is in e.g. terza

2. You stringer on the inside, they disengage to strike you in the face (this is just like Plate 7)

3. Parry with your dagger high over your sword arm,

4. While cutting them in the thigh, or thrusting them in the armpit (gently).

Plate 25
https://guywindsor.net/blog/rbc410

Notes

Plate 38

FIGURE THAT STRIKES WITH A STRAMAZZONE RIVERSO IN THE FACE OF A LEFT-HANDER AND WILL ALSO BE ABLE TO STRIKE HIM In The Chest In Seconda; Or Alternately In Quarta From The Outside Of The Enemy's Sword During The Disengage That His Point Makes In Order To Strike.

The adversary, who will be left handed, lying in quarta with his arm extended, you will begin to stringer his sword inside in terza, with your dagger high, and he disengaging in order to strike you in seconda in the face, you will be able to strike him in three manners: first, only lowering your dagger and parrying his sword you will strike him with a stramazzone riverso in the face; alternately, in seconda in the chest; taking note, nonetheless, that during his disengage it could be better to strike him in with your sword alone on the outside.

One of the more pernicious myths surrounding historical fencing is the idea that people weren't allowed to be left-handed back in the old days. In fact, trying to train children out of left-handedness came in and out of fashion, from place to place. So it was sometimes true in some places (my own grandmother, for instance, was almost certainly left-handed, but trained to use her right), but not generally true, and you should certainly use whichever hand you're most comfortable with, and once you are proficient with one hand, you should train to use the other, as it offers a useful learning opportunity. This goes triple for teachers.

Left-handers fence a lot of right-handers, which means they get used to that situation. Unless you have only one training partner and they happen to be left-handed, you need to seek out lefties to fence against (whichever hand you use). Otherwise, you'll be fencing in an unfamiliar situation, while they're slap bang in the middle of their comfort zone.

In this plate, I want you to take both parts, and practice it both ways – so right-handed v.

left-handed (righty wins), and left-handed v. right handed (lefty wins). This means there are four iterations of the drill:

	Drill Type	You	Partner	Actions:
1	Basic	Right-handed	Left-handed	You stringer, they attack, you strike
2	Basic other way	Right-handed	Left-handed	They stringer, you attack, they strike
3	Reversed	Left-handed	Right-handed	You stringer, they attack, you strike
4	Reversed other way	Left-handed	Right-handed	They stringer, you attack, they strike

The pattern of the drill is simple. In its "basic" set-up:

1. You (right-handed, in terza, dagger high) stringer your partner (left-handed, in quarta), on your outside, their inside

2. Partner disengages to strike you in the face in seconda,

3. You parry with the dagger under your sword arm, and stramazzone to their face, or thrust to the chest in seconda. Alternatively, play it exactly like Plate 16, parrying and striking with the sword alone, in one tempo.

Plate 38
https://guywindsor.net/blog/rbc411

Notes

Plate 39

FIGURE THAT PARRIES THE HEAD WITH THE POINT OF THE SWORD HIGH AND WITH THE DAGGER CROSSED WITH HIS SWORD On The Inside At The Forte, So That The Same Will Be Able To Strike In Two Manners: First With A Thrust To The Face; Or Alternately With A Riverso To The Leg

I would certainly have wronged myself if I had not revealed to you this noble parry, or defence, which defends, and saves such a noble part of the body; accordingly on his occasion I put forth to you the present figures, of whom one lies in prima, and the other in quinta; and from quinta, only by raising his arm and turning his hand into quarta, increasing the pace, he will have come to gain the sword of the adversary on the inside, and the enemy disengaging by turning under his enemy's sword, he will have thrown a dritto fendente at the same, but the same only by turning his hand into seconda with the point high, putting the dagger to the rear on the forte of his sword, will be able to strike the adversary safely in two places: with a thrust in the face, or a cut to the leg, as the two lines descending from the point of the sword demonstrate well, the one falling to the head, and the other to the thigh.

Be honest with me – if I wrote like that, would you buy my books?
I thought not.
The one does this, the other that, who which what how?
It's fortunately a very simple play.

1. You are in quinta, your partner in prima,

2. You stringer them on the inside,

3. Your partner disengages to cut you in the head with a dritto fendente,

4. You parry by turning your hand to seconda and raising your sword,

5. And at the same time crossing your dagger behind your sword (so, between your face and your weapon),

6. Keeping their sword on your dagger, you can thrust them directly in the face (I turn my hand to quarta to do that), or cut to their leg (with a roverso).

I used an image of this parry to promote my Complete Rapier Course, and it generated some interesting negative feedback; one or two people who are clearly much better at rapier than Capoferro (and all the other historical masters) claimed that it was a stupid thing to do, because your opponent can just rush in and stab you with the dagger. This is true if you fall fast asleep after your parry. Instead of taking a nap, parry and strike immediately, and stay alert. If your opponent is the rushing-in kind, then you may need to take a step back. Good thing you've been practising your footwork, huh?

Plate 39
https://guywindsor.net/blog/rbc412

We have covered a lot of material in this class. Your base just got a lot broader. I would strongly recommend using what you have learned in Workbook Three regarding how to train, to get that base deeper and more solid, before carrying on to the next class. The rule of c's, add a step, coaching, and so on.

Take your time, and move on when what we have covered so far is becoming a natural part of your skillset, not something you have to work to recall.

Notes

THE FIFTEENTH CLASS

COMPLETE THE BASICS

Warm up as usual, and run through your basics, including the Footwork Form, Hunt the Debole, and Plates 7 and 16. Spend some time on the wall target and the pell as well, if you have them.

Now run through those basics again, but with the other hand. This may take a while. From now on, you should be spending at least a few minutes in every session using the 'wrong' hand.

Recall from book two that I asked you to reconstruct several plates from the source alone. It's time to do that again, with the rapier and dagger plates 26, 27, and 28.

As before, I'll provide the text and pictures, and I am eagerly waiting for you to send me a video of you doing *your* interpretation of these actions. And of course if you get stuck, feel free to get in touch.

Plate 26

15

A FIGURE THAT PARRIES WITH THE SWORD IN QUARTA ACCOMPANIED WITH THE DAGGER AND STRIKES IN QUARTA TO The Face Or With A Riverso To The Arm As The Figure Shows

If it so happens that you find yourself in an extended terza with the dagger at your wrist, your adversary being in whatsoever guard apt for stringering on the outside, you will commence to stringer him with the same terza, now high, now low, according to the occasion, however without moving the dagger from its place, and your adversary disengaging to strike you in quarta or seconda, parrying in quarta with your sword accompanied with your dagger you will be able to strike him, as you see, either with a riverso to the arm or a quarta to the face.

Plate 27

A FIGURE THAT MAKES A FEINT ABOVE THE DAGGER, AND, THE ADVERSARY RAISING TO PARRY THE SAME, STRIKES HIM IN The Chest In Quarta, Disengaging The Sword Under

Finding yourself in an extended terza with the dagger at the wrist, and the adversary being in a low quarta with his sword withdrawn and his dagger high and extended, you will commence to make a feint above his dagger in terza; maintaining your dagger in its place, he parrying upwards with his dagger, wanting to strike you in the same tempo in quarta or seconda, you will disengage under, and parrying his attack therewith you will strike him in quarta in the chest.

Notes

Plate 28

FIGURE THAT PARRIES UNDER HIS RIGHT ARM WITH THE DAGGER, AND STRIKES IN SECONDA INTO THE FACE Or With A Stramazzone Riverso In The Sword Arm

Lying in a low or high terza, with your dagger at your wrist, your adversary being in whatsoever guard convenient to stringer on the outside, you will begin to stringer on the outside in high or low terza, according to the occasion, elevating your dagger, and he wanting to disengage to the inside, and throw in quarta or seconda, you, parrying down with the dagger under your sword arm, will throw at him a stramazzone to his arm or you will strike him in seconda in the face, as is shown.

Notes

What now?

At this stage you should have a working interpretation of these three plates. I hope it's clear that none of them is nearly as complex as either of our core games, Hunt the Debole or the Dagger Parrying Game.

Now what I would like you to do is choose one of them, and become proficient in its execution. Run it through all the complexity generators that you know (you can look them up in Workbook Three), and take it from "I know the choreography" to "I can actually do it at speed against a non-compliant partner". Good luck!

Notes

THE SIXTEENTH CLASS

OTHER WEAPONS

Begin as usual: warm up, run through the basics, do a little remedial work to get you into an "I'm deliberately improving my skills" frame of mind, remember to work your off-hand, and do some slow fencing, and then we'll move on.

The dagger is arguably the most common accompanying weapon to the sword in this period. It is not the only one though. A bare left hand is vulnerable in a sword fight, so one can use literally anything to protect it, and to act as a secondary weapon. A chair, a large beer mug, a lantern, a cape, a hat, a stick, anything.

Vincentio Saviolo in his book *His Practice*, published in 1595, wrote:

"I will tell you, this weapon must bee used with a glove, and if a man should be without a glove, it were better to hazard a little hurt of the hand, thereby to become maister of his enemies Swoorde, than to breake with the swoord, and so give his enemy the advantage of him.

Moreover, having the use of your lefte hand, and wearing a gantlet or glove of maile, your enemy shall no sooner make a thrust, but you shal be readye to catch his swoorde fast, and to command him at your pleasure: wherefore I wish you not to defend any thrust with the swoorde, because in so dooing you loose the point."

He is explicitly describing a maille glove for the left hand ("chain mail"), which he recommends the use of. The Royal Armouries in Leeds has one on display – with the maille covering the palm and inside of the fingers, but not the back of the hand. But Saviolo is also explicit that you should parry with your left hand even if you don't have a glove. Capoferro describes a bare-handed hand parry on plate 14.

Cape

Of all the possible accompaniments, a cloak or cape (a short cloak) is the next most common after the dagger, and Capoferro includes a couple of plates of cape and sword play, Plates 36 and 37. Plate 36 includes instruction on how to get the cape off your shoulder and onto your left arm (right for left-handers).

It's worth remembering that in this period a cape was as normal as a jacket is to us. You have put a jacket on and taken it off hundreds of times, and don't even think about it as a skill. Parents of small children know how much of a learned skill dressing and undressing really is. To begin with the cape will feel ungainly and awkward, but with practice it should become second nature to slip it off and onto your arm, ready to parry with. All Capoferro says about that is this:

having the cape thereabout, it will be allowed to fall down off the right shoulder, to as far as the middle of the left arm, and then wrapping the left hand to the outside, enveloping the arm in the said cape, putting oneself with it into terza, or in some other guard as you like.

You may find a video helpful:

Holding the Cape (from plate 36)
https://guywindsor.net/blog/rbc413

Plate 36, part one

This plate has not a lot of data in the image, but a wealth of options in the text, all starting from you both being in terza. They are:

1. You partner cuts at your head. You pass forwards, parrying with the cape-covered arm, while thrusting them in the chest.

2. Your partner cuts at your head. You advance the front foot, parrying with your sword (in guardia di testa, which is prima done with the point across, so your sword guards your head) and your caped arm together, and cut a mandritto to their head.

3. Your partner cuts your head. You pass forwards, parrying with your sword in guardia di testa accompanied by the caped arm (as in 2), and cut to their leg with a step of the right foot.

4. Your partner cuts a mandritto at your leg. Slip and cut their arm with a roverso, just like in Plate 8.

5. Your partner cuts a roverso at your leg. Slip and cut their arm with a mandritto.

6. Or the "best way": your partner cuts at you (it could be to the head or leg, the text is not clear). Parry with the sword, and keep control of their sword with your caped arm, and riposte (how is also not specified).

I have split these up into two videos. Part one has options 1-3, defences against the cut to the head. Part two has options 4-6, dealing with cuts to the leg.

Notes

Plate 36 part one
https://guywindsor.net/blog/rbc414

Plate 36 part two
https://guywindsor.net/blog/rbc415

16

Notes

Plate 37

This plate has rather less material on it, but clearly shows controlling the opponent's sword with your caped arm. The play is like so:

1. Your opponent is in quarta. You approach them, stringering them on the inside, with your caped arm under the forte of your sword.

2. As your opponent disengages to attack, parry up with your caped arm, while counter-disengaging in quarta to thrust them in the face.

Plate 37
https://guywindsor.net/blog/rbc416

Notes

Throwing the Cape

Capoferro does not discuss this. But have you noticed how I snuck a Saviolo quote into the beginning of this chapter, and now am dropping in something from Alfieri?

This is because your study of Capoferro is a great base for mastering rapier swordsmanship. But it's very important that you see beyond your core style or core source, and out into the wider world. There is some amazing stuff out there that Capoferro didn't include. It would be a shame to miss it.

Francesco Ferdinando Alfieri was (according to his fencing treatise *La Scherma* (*Fencing,*1640)) a master-at-arms to the Accademia Delia in Padua. His works also include La Bandiera (The Banner, a treatise on messaging with flags) published in 1638, and La Picca (The Pike), published in 1641.

La Scherma was reprinted in 1646, and released in a new edition in 1653 titled *L'arte di ben maneggiare la spada* ("The Art of Handling the Sword Well"), which adds a section on the spadone.

My school T-shirt has had a plate from Alfieri on the back since 2001. He's that good! And here he shows throwing the cape onto the opponent's sword to weigh it down before stabbing him.

The trick to it is how you hold the cape – if it is tightly wrapped round your arm, you can't throw it.

Throwing the Cape, from Alfieri
https://guywindsor.net/blog/rbc417

Notes

CONCLUSION

My goal in writing this workbook is to provide you with all the information you *need* to become proficient in rapier and dagger play. It may not include all the information you *want*. If I have stimulated your curiosity, that's all to the good. And looking back at this series of workbooks as a whole, we have certainly covered every common rapier action, every type of play, and there should be nothing in the entire corpus of rapier material spanning two centuries that you cannot grasp, so long as you can find an adequate source that you can actually read.

For further information about researching swordsmanship, creating syllabi from your research, running a club, teaching, and everything else, read my book *The Theory and Practice of Historical Martial Arts*. You can get a free copy of the book in PDF format by signing up to my mailing list here:

Theory and Practice
https://guywindsor.net/blog/rbc418

If 'proper' books are your thing, then you should probably get the Duellist's Companion.

The Duellist's Companion
https://guywindsor.net/blog/rbctdc

If you prefer video instruction, then The Essential Rapier Course (from which many of the videos in this workbook came) might suit you better.

You can use this link to get 50% off the regular price for the Essential Rapier Course:

There are of course many other instructors out there whose approach you may enjoy and benefit from, so don't feel obliged to limit yourself to just mine.

GLOSSARY

The table below includes words that are either unique to fencing sources, or have a specific technical meaning in a fencing context. The translations are not necessarily applicable to modern Italian or other historical sources.

Italian grammar is quite simple, but has some aspects that English speakers may find odd - not least that a single word may have different forms, and to make a word plural, we can't just throw an 's' on the end. In general, nouns are either masculine or feminine, and adjectives will have both masculine and feminine forms that agree with the noun they describe. For example: quarta guardia, fourth guard; filo falso, false edge.

In general:

Nouns ending in -e when singular will end in -i when plural: fendente, fendenti.
Nouns ending in -o when singular will end in -i when plural: colpo, colpi.
Nouns ending in -a when singular will end in -e when plural: ligadura, ligadure.

Italian	English	Comments
Accrescere	To step forwards	without passing.
Cavazione	disengage	
Colpo/i	a blow or strike.	
Contratempo	countertime	see Plate 11.
Debole	weak. The second half of the blade (towards the point).	
Dritto, diritto, derito	Right, forehand or true.	*Filo* or *taglio dritto* is the true edge.
Falso	False edge, back edge.	
Fendente	Descending blow.	Usually qualified by *mandritto / dritto* (forehand) or *roverso* (backhand).
Forte	Strong, the first half of the blade (towards the hilt).	
Imbroccata	imbroccata	A thrust in prima, with the point lower than the hand.
Mandritto	Forehand.	See *dritto/diritto*.

Passo	A pass, also the length of a passing step, also the space between your feet when standing.	
Prima	First. Guard position, above the shoulder.	
Quarta	Fourth. Guard position, on the inside.	
Ricavazione	Redisengage	A second disengage, used to counter a contracavazione (counterdisengage).
Riverso / roverso	Backhand.	
Rotella	Rotella. A kind of shield.	
Sbasso	A low void	as on Plate 11, but not Capoferro's term.
Scanso del pie dritto	Void of the right foot	from Plate 17.
Scanso della vita	Void of the waist	from Plate 19.
Seconda	Second. Guard position level with the shoulder.	
Stoccata	A rising thrust, usually with the hand in terza.	
Strada	Way.	This is used in the sense of the direct line between the two combatants. Hence to step *fora di strada*, "out of the way", is to step off the line.
Stramazone	A whirling blow from the wrist.	
Stretto / stretta / strette	constrained	past participle of 'stringere'
Stretto / stretta / strette	Close, constrained, narrow.	Used to refer to a guard held with the point forwards in the rotella section.
Stringere	To constrain	Generally synonymous with find or gain the sword.
Taglio/e	Cut, but also cutting edge.	
Tempo/i	Time.	A motion done in measure; an opportunity to strike. Also 'rhythm'.
Terza	Third. Guard position, held low and in the middle.	Can be inside or outside the lead thigh.
Tondo	"Round": A horizontal blow	

THANKS

This workbook series did not spring straight from my brain to the printed page; many people helped along the way. Curtis Fee produced the graphic elements and initial cover design, using my school logo as envisioned by Titta Tolvanen. Rob Simpson also helped with cover design, and Bek Pickard took my crappy layout and made it professional. My mum proof-read the final text. Many of the video clips feature my student Maaret Sirkkala, and were shot using Deveril's awesome camera.

The images from *Gran Simulacro* were photos I took with the help of James Hester and Malcolm Fare, from the latter's own copy of the book. The photos were then cleaned up by Alexander Craddock.

My interpretation of Capoferro owes much to Sean Hayes, Devon Boorman, William Wilson, Jherek Swanger, Jared Kirby, Tom Leoni, and my students Tanda Tuovinen, Maaret Sirkkala, Janne Högdahl, Jaana Wessman, Orava Wessman, Topi Mikkola, Otto Kopra, and countless others who have shown up to my classes and inspired me to do better.

FURTHER READING

If you've enjoyed this book you should definitely visit my blog (at guywindsor.net/blog), and sign up for my mailing list. It's populated only by the excellent, there's never any spam, and members get the news first about new releases and giveaways. You may also like the following:

The Duellist's Companion
A training manual for 17th century Italian rapier. This is still the standard work on the interpretation and practice of Capoferro's rapier system.

The Theory and Practice of Historical Martial Arts
This book includes all seven instalments of *The Swordsman's Quick Guide,* as well as extensive instruction on recreating historical martial arts from historical sources, how to train, how to teach, even how to get better sleep.

The *Swordsman's Quick Guide* Series

The Swordsman's Quick Guide Series, volume 1: The Seven Principles of Mastery. This instalment covers the principles you can follow to attain mastery in any field. It lays the groundwork for everything. And it's free on all platforms!

The Swordsman's Quick Guide Series, volume 2: Choosing a Sword. This instalment offers advice and guidance for choosing a sword, including the specifications for a range of historical sword types.

The Swordsman's Quick Guide, volume 3: Preparing for Freeplay. This instalment covers how to get from set basic drills to freeplay, by increasing complexity in a consistent and constructive way.

The Swordsman's Quick Guide, volume 4: Ethics. This instalment gives readers the basic tools to establish for themselves the ethical dimension of martial arts training.

The Swordsman's Quick Guide, volume 5: How to Teach a Basic Class. This instalment is intended for people just starting out as teachers, to give them the teaching knowledge and confidence to run a safe basic class.

The Swordsman's Quick Guide, volume 6: Fencing Theory. This instalment covers what fencing theory is, how it works, and how you can use it effectively in your study of swordsmanship. This is also available in the free 70-page sample of *The Theory and Practice of Historical Martial Arts.*

The Swordsman's Quick Guide, volume 7: Breathing. This instalment is a detailed examination of breathing training, drawing from many sources and including instruction in my basic breathing practices, with links to instructional videos for each exercise.

And if you're interested in more than just the rapier, you should try these:

The Swordsman's Companion, a training manual for medieval longsword
This was my first book, and it has become something of a classic in this field. As a training manual, it is largely replaced by *The Medieval Longsword*, but as a book about how and why to train, it is still relevant.

The *Mastering the Art of Arms* Series

Mastering the Art of Arms vol 1: The Medieval Dagger, a training manual for Fiore's dagger material. This is a complete overview of the dagger material in Fiore's art of arms, and includes instruction on how to fall, and how to develop real skills, as well as covering all of the fundamental attacks with and defences against the dagger.

Mastering the Art of Arms vol 2: The Medieval Longsword, a training manual for Fiore's longsword material. If you want to learn how to train and fight with a longsword in an authentic medieval style, this book is for you. This book features an introduction by the excellent historical novelist and medieval combatant Christian Cameron.

Mastering the Art of Arms, vol 3: Advanced Longsword, Form and Function. This covers using forms for skill development, and a lot of Fiore-specific training, building on the groundwork laid in *The Medieval Longsword*.

Swordfighting for Writers, Game Designers, and Martial Artists
This book is made up of about 50% posts from my blog, and 50% new material, and does exactly what it says in the title. It also features an introduction from the one and only Neal Stephenson, author of *Snow Crash*, *The Diamond Age*, and *The Baroque Cycle*, to name but a few.

The Art of Sword Fighting in Earnest
This is an accurate translation of Filippo Vadi's *De Arte Gladiatoria Dimicandi*, with a detailed introduction, commentary from a practical swordsmanship perspective, and a full glossary. This book was examined as part of my PhD, so it's been academically vetted at the highest level.

Finally, let me ask you now to review this book, for better or worse, wherever is convenient for you. If I've done something right I need to know, to do it again; moreover, I need to know what could be improved. To paraphrase Vadi: "And if this little work of mine finds its way into the hands of anyone versed in the art, and appears to them to have anything redundant or wrong, may it please them to cut, take away or add to it as they please. Because in the end I place myself under their correction and judgement."
Thank you!

Guy Windsor, Ipswich, March 27th 2019.